Retro

Focus on Contemporary Issues (FOCI) addresses the pressing problems, ideas and debates of the new millennium. Subjects are drawn from the arts, sciences and humanities, and are linked by the impact they have had or are having on contemporary culture. FOCI books are intended for an intelligent, alert audience with a general understanding of, and curiosity about, the intellectual debates shaping culture today. Instead of easing readers into a comfortable awareness of particular fields, these books are combative. They offer points of view, take sides and are written with passion.

SERIES EDITORS
Barrie Bullen and Peter Hamilton

In the same series

Retro

The Culture of Revival

ELIZABETH E. GUFFEY

REAKTION BOOKS

For Ellen

Published by Reaktion Books Ltd
33 Great Sutton Street
London EC1V 0DX, UK

www.reaktionbooks.co.uk

First published 2006

Printed and bound in Great Britain
by Cromwell Press, Trowbridge, Wiltshire

British Library Cataloguing in Publishing Data
Guffey, Elizabeth E.
    Retro: the culture of revival. – (Focus on contemporary issues)
    1. Popular culture – History   2. Memory – Social aspects
    3. Nostalgia   4. Clothing and dress – Social aspects   5. Fashion – Social aspects
    6. Design – History   7. Retromarketing
    I. Title
    306

    ISBN-13: 9 781 86189 290 4
    ISBN-10: 1 86189 290 X

Contents

Remembering When We Were Modern

When the Victoria and Albert Museum in London opened its summer exhibition season in 1966, it was little prepared for the rush and hype that would surround its retrospective of an obscure nineteenth-century draughtsman and illustrator. Yet in just four months more than 100,000 visitors thronged to a survey of the work of Aubrey Beardsley – more than for any exhibit of prints or drawings in living memory. The exhibition attracted viewers who were egged on by word of mouth and the scent of scandal: on the charge of obscene content, the Metropolitan Police seized Beardsley prints from a shop near the museum soon after the show opened. Huge lines formed to view the Victoria & Albert Museum's suddenly infamous collection of leering satyrs, wilting youths and full-bodied giantesses who cavorted in unusual, often insinuating, poses. Writing in *Art News*, John Russell described a public 'stirred in many cases by reports of phallic enormities and fanstastications [*sic*] of the anal orifice . . . and it must be said that they were not altogether disappointed'.[1] The nearly antique Beardsley, who never had an exhibition during his lifetime, was hailed as 'the new hero in London'.[2]

Beardsley's posthumous exhibition offered harmless excitement and an intoxicating whiff of official disapproval, a sensibility that also pervaded Beatles' concerts, the adoption of the miniskirt and other popular trends of the period. Like Beatlemania, an 'Art Nouveau fever' infected popular culture in Western Europe and North America;[3] in 1964 *Time* magazine airily declared that 'the revival of Art Nouveau' had arrived, its forms 'old and yet new'.[4] The revival of interest in Art Nouveau that culminated in the 1960s was evidenced in forms ranging from scholarly museum exhibitions to mass-produced wallpaper. Moreover, as popular culture in the 1960s began to change, the remnants of this musty 80-year-old movement became the syntax of sexy, youthful rebellion. The older style was a boon to image-conscious graphic designers, spawning a wave of swaying, shimmying typography and illustration that enriched popular and artistic icons. The intertwining of this late nineteenth-century art and design movement with the 1960s counter-culture led *Time* magazine in 1967 to rename San Francisco, a Mecca for youthful chic, 'Nouveau Frisco'.

Superficially, this rediscovery appeared to echo the resurrection of other movements and styles in the history of art. The rehabilitation of Beardsley, however, as well as the Art Nouveau movement in general, was pervaded with a new sensibility that separates it from nineteenth-century revivalism. Beardsley and the Art Nouveau period lacked the aura of misty medievalism or the authority of antiquity that informed the Gothic and Classical Revivals of the previous century. The resurgence of interest in the art and design of the late nineteenth century suggests the beginning of a unique post-war tendency: a popular thirst for the recovery of earlier, and yet still modern, periods at an ever-accelerating rate. But this tendency should not be dismissed as merely a series of reflexive stylistic gestures. Instead, it might be more usefully seen as representing a kind of subversion in which the artistic and cultural vanguard began looking backwards in order to go forwards. These groups saw their approach towards the past spread quickly. And yet the extension of these ideas was also a sort of inoculation for the greater mainstream. The historian Fredric Jameson has suggested that as society has developed it has found new ways to tell itself its own history.[5] Retro allows us to come to terms with the modern past.

A Word with Many Meanings

As Voltaire noted, history does not change, but what we want from it does. 'Retro' carries a pervasive, if somewhat imprecise, meaning; gradually creeping into daily usage over the past thirty years, there have been few attempts to define it. Used to describe cultural predisposition and personal taste, technological obsolescence and mid-century style, 'retro's' neologism rolls off the tongue with an ease that transcends slang. Although the term is of recent vintage, it can also describe the atmosphere at the Beardsley exhibition of 1966 and its aftermath. While words like 'fad', 'fashion' and 'revival' swirled around the resurrected Art Nouveau style, 'retro' acquired its current connotations in the early 1970s. Although retro is easily dismissed as a backwards glance at the past, the nuances underlying its appeal are often overlooked.

'Retro' can serve as little more than a trendy synonym for 'old-fashioned' or simply 'old'. Monaco's Tourism Office, for instance, recently repackaged a standard tour that included visits to the Principality's wax museum and an exhibition of Napoleonic memorabilia as 'Retro Day: A History and Tradition Tour'. At its best, this form of 'retro' functions much like 'timeless' or 'classic' as cultural advertising; 'retro' products, places or ideas can assume an iconic status, denoting an undefined time gone by. Carrying deep emotional appeal, this form of 'retro' embraces shopping malls that evoke an ageless High Street, as well as recipes taken from family cookbooks.

Nevertheless, the word can also serve as shorthand for a period style situated in the immediate post-war years. In the USA, 'retro' frequently describes American material culture at mid-century, encompassing saddle shoes and tail fins, Eames furniture and suburban ranch houses. Embraced by collectors and nostalgia buffs alike, this form of 'retro' can stretch to include the influence of the 1950s and '60s on contemporary forms, including the updated BMW Mini and Volkswagen's new Beetle. Yet the term is also applied to 1950s subcultures: Polynesian-inspired 'Tiki' instrumental pop or lounge music as well as the T-shirt-and-leather-jacket style favoured by juvenile delinquents.

'Retro' can also describe an outlook on life. It may suggest a predisposition or inherent social conservatism that cleaves to the values and mores of the past, identified in the popular press with such social phenomena as home schooling and an embrace of traditional gender roles. More than a quest for a simpler life, this 'retro' attitude also carries a darker suspicion that recent social, cultural and political developments are profoundly corrosive.

'Retro' can also suggest technological obsolescence: manual typewriters and cash registers have become 'retro'. Even more, gadgets that once defined the text and texture of modern consumer technology, including eight-track tape decks and bulky cordless phones, now carry a 'retro' cachet. Entire subcultures devoted to outmoded technological apparatuses have developed: the adherents of retro gaming, for instance, reconfigure obsolete video games to play on today's computers, while others restore the old computers to enjoy the 'original' game experience. With irrelevance sought out for its own sake, 'retro' transcends period styles or personal predisposition.

'Retro' has been dismissed as a fashionable novelty and fodder for popular culture's relentless appetite, but its most potent connotation is often overlooked: 'retro' suggests a fundamental shift in the popular relationship with the past. Beyond presenting older forms with an Indian summer of novelty, 'retro' ignores remote lore and focuses on the recent past. It ignores, for instance, the Middle Ages or classical antiquity. Half-

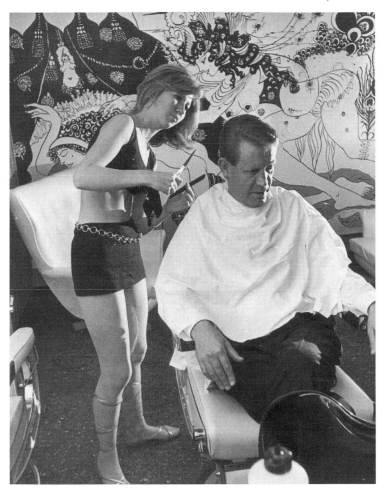

A scantily-clad female at work in the Samson and Delilah barbers, where the walls are decorated with Beardsley-inspired murals, c. 1966.

ironic, half-longing, 'retro' considers the recent past with an unsentimental nostalgia. It is unconcerned with the sanctity of tradition or reinforcing social values; indeed, it often insinuates a form of subversion while side-stepping historical accuracy. In 1966 the bikini-clad, all-female staff of the

Samson and Delilah barbers in London gave a winking nod to a nine-teenth-century world of erotic fantasy when they offered haircuts in a salon decorated with Beardsley-inspired murals. Retro quotes styles from the past, but applies them in anomalous settings; it regards the past from a bemused distance, its dark humour re-mixing popular mid-century drinks and serving them up as 'atomic cocktails'. Casting a glance backwards, to older but still modern periods, retro eludes the positivist progressivism that inflected the 'Modern' era. Even more fundamentally, it gently nudges us away from older ideas of 'Modernity' and towards an uncharted future. The culture of revival has changed.

The Deviant Revival

In 1962 John Glenn became the first American to orbit the earth. Upon his re-entry into the Earth's atmosphere, however, the ceramic heat shield on his capsule came unlatched. If the shield came off, he would die in the 4000°F heat outside. To reduce this risk, the mission control scientists decided not to jettison the set of rockets positioned just above the shield, which were normally abandoned during re-entry; they hoped that the rockets' metal straps would keep it attached. The 'retro-pack' remained in place, but disintegrated in flaming chunks as the capsule re-entered the atmosphere. Public and officials alike watched in horror, believing that the craft itself was burning. After Glenn's successful splashdown, however, his 'retro rockets' made their way into popular speech.

'Retro' thus entered the public imagination with the space-age lexicon of the early 1960s. 'Retro rockets' provided an all-important opposite thrust, turning space probes into orbit or, as in Glenn's case, slowing a rocket's descent to earth. Little used before the nineteenth century, 'retro' was adopted to suggest a powerful counter to forward propulsion. Until the post-war years 'retro' functioned primarily as a prefix; its closest relative, 'retrograde', referred to planetary rotations that deviated from the usual direction of celestial bodies. Only in the late twentieth century did 'retro' gain associations that would set it in opposition to the positivism of the space programme and the applied science of the nineteenth century. Retro came to symbolize a deviant form of revivalism.

All cultural forms and expressions inevitably take something from the past, but revivalism is intimately linked to the nineteenth-century. At that time, systematic approaches to history forced study of the past to become professionalized, creating entire disciplines, like archaeology and geology, and a broader awareness of the past seeped into other scholarly fields as well. As historical styles and periods were identified and differentiated, artists, designers and architects delved into them to help express serious contemporary themes like nationalism and morality. From paintings like the Wallace Collection's *Henri III and the Ambassadors* (1827–28) by the British artist Richard Parkes Bonnington to the false clapboards of Colonial Revival homes, faith and nationhood were evoked in historically accurate detail. For the architect A.W.N. Pugin, buildings in the Gothic style seemed to embody the spirituality that he sought in his own life, and the Gothic Revival paralleled his embrace of Roman Catholicism. Byzantine buildings provided a source of inspiration to architects in the Balkans, which had only recently emerged from Turkish rule. In Spain the Mudéjar Revival recalled the country's Islamic roots and graced churches and bullfight rings.

Unlike nineteenth-century revivalism, which found its roots in the misty realms of the distant past, retro does not glance nostalgically at pre-industrial times. Any fascination with forms of art and design associated with the Industrial Revolution and its aftermath would have left earlier revivalists like Pugin speechless with disbelief. Retro, however, champions such styles as these, highlighting the artistic and popular culture of the industrial age that the earlier reformers so often overlooked. It is suffused with an ambivalent view of Modernity and challenges positivist views of technology, industry and, most of all, of progress itself. Rather than evading the symptoms of Modernity like so much of nineteenth-century revivalism, retro is an attempt to come to terms with Modernity's ideas, as well as its boundaries and even its mortality.

Older forms of revivalism would be unequal to this challenge; retro detachment, perhaps the phenomenon's most enduring quality, highlights its ironic stance. The seriousness of purpose that shaped older revivals destabilizes retro's non-serious and subversive instincts. Retro does not seek out proud examples of the past; it shuffles instead through history's unopened closets and unlit corners. Highlighting popular culture, it has adopted post-war American 'Googie' coffee-shop architecture and gangster-style pinstripe suits as easily as Eames chairs and Bauhaus type. But retro's non-seriousness should be distinguished from frivolity.

'Retro' began to evoke the recent past in the early 1970s, when it was used to characterize the work of a coterie of Parisian film critics, writers and fashion designers. The growing genre of films and literature that examined themes of resistance to, as well as collaboration with, the Nazis during World War Two was dubbed the 'mode rétro'. A generation too young to remember the war years embraced films like Louis Malle's *Lacombe Lucien* (1974), which presented the Third Reich in moodily atmospheric terms that neither condemned nor endorsed their subject. The stylish treatment of the war years in these films, however, seemed to many to be analogous to the crisp trench coats and war-era platform shoes that by the early 1970s had appeared in both Parisian fashion houses and flea markets. What began as a challenge to Gaullist interpretations of resistance during the Nazi occupation turned into a fashionable trend that deliberately mingled decadent and libertarian allusions.

By the late 1970s a fashion-conscious yet highly irreverent version of 'retro' crept into English, where its meaning remained fluid and vaguely negative; for many it represented a desire to recycle the past in a somewhat exploitative manner. Using the space-age jargon of the Kennedy era, in an article of 1979 titled 'Will the "Retro" Look Make It?', the fashion journalist

Bernardine Morris reported that 'after a number of years during which fashion was perceived as having made tremendous progress in the direction of freedom, comfort and style, the forward thrust' of design was 'aborted'.[6] But the early use of 'retro' in fashion and film circles was quickly expanded in the following decade. In 'Hot Potatoes: Art and Politics in 1980', the critic Lucy Lippard fearfully announced the arrival of 'retrochic' in the art world, describing the phenomenon as a 'reactionary wolf in counter-cultural sheep's clothing'. For Lippard, 'retro' was a form of avant-garde stylishness employed by contemporary artists who featured 'sexist, heterosexist, classist and racist violence' in their work.[7] Lippard described as 'retro' those artists who embraced socially unacceptable attitudes as libertarian gestures, including a Canadian rock group that called itself the 'Battered Wives' and Donald Newman's exhibit of 1979 at Artists Space of abstract works on paper titled 'Nigger Drawings'. As a symbol of resistance to the political and social certainties of the mainstream, Lippard equated 'retro' with that other phenomenon of mid-1970s rebellion: punk rock. Nevertheless, she noted that retrochic did not contain 'the harsh Brechtian irony' that could be found among British working-class punks; rather, 'retro' transgression merely used its audience as parents to be rebelled against.[8] Whether represented by Yves Saint Laurent, who sent couture models down the Paris catwalks in clothes modelled on war-era prostitutes, or Sid Vicious, who wore a red swastika T-shirt while cruising Jewish neighbourhoods in Paris, 'retro' attracted attention in Europe and America in the 1970s. Ultimately, however, it was the proliferation of Postmodern thought in the 1980s that gave 'retro' a more sustained meaning. Where Lippard rooted retrochic in acrimonious if amoral rebellion, even calling an article in the *Village Voice* 'Retrochic, Looking Back in Anger',[9] Postmodern theorists embraced 'retro' as an example of culture's transformation in the wake of mass media. In 'History: A Retro Scenario', a chapter in his *Simulacra and Simulation* (1981), Jean Baudrillard described the 'death pangs of the real and of the rational' in contemporary culture.[10] Examining recent cinema for manifestations of this new 'retro' sensibility, he identified a series of popular historical films, including Roman Polanski's *Chinatown* (1974) and Stanley Kubrick's *Barry Lyndon* (1975), which re-create the past with what he saw as a 'disquieting' perfection.[11] Peter Bogdanovich's *The Last Picture Show* (1971) so closely imitated the 'customs in and the atmosphere of the American small town' that a casually 'distracted' viewer like himself 'would have . . . thought it to be an original production from the 1950s'. Upon closer scrutiny, however, the film rouses 'just a slight suspicion: it was a little too good, more in tune . . . without the psychological, moral, and sentimental blotches of the films of that era'. In the end, this 'hyperrealist restitution of 1950s cinema' embodies Baudrillard's 'retro', a series of empty representational forms that can simulate only earlier, lost forms of reality.

Baudrillard, like the earlier *mode rétro* critics, still linked 'retro' closely with the evanescent lens of the movie camera; here he found a cinematic stylishness that suggested the 'real' was in decline. A sense of an amoral emptiness, malaise, decline and dislocation – a kind of self-indulgent nostalgia – has haunted commentators on the subject in general. But in the past twenty years, since Baudrillard's commentary, 'retro' has continued to evolve in meaning. From the opening in 1986 of American Retro, a London gift shop specializing in clothing and memorabilia, to the historian Philip Meggs's promotion at the end of the decade of a graphic-design movement called Retro, which was led by New York-based designers, the implications of the word 'retro' were expanding.[12]

While Baudrillard presented 'retro' as essentially content-less, more recently the British historian Raphael Samuel judged it an 'unofficial form of knowledge'. In *Theatres of Memory* (1994) he analysed the symptoms of 'retrochic' through a series of eclectic expressions that have flourished in the last forty years, ranging from kinky clothes and souvenir ceramics to 'country kitchens' and re-mixes of 1960s 'classic' rock music. Samuel nudged 'retro' down from the cinema screen and fashion catwalk, prowling instead around flea-market stands and shelter magazines, trendy gift shops and upscale diners to survey its impact. Above all, his retrochic represented a populist phenomenon; a sensibility that sidestepped established historical accounts and questions of chronology and context, Samuel's 'retrochic' made room for historicist fantasy in everyday life.[13]

Fascinated with a 'retro' fusion of old and new, Samuel focused on flea-market pub mirrors decorated with silkscreened simulations of cut glass and gingham and pine 'country kitchens' powered by state-of-the-art electric appliances. As Baudrillard would have it, however, such re-creations are 'a little too good', a little too contemporary in their consciousness. Like Lippard, Samuel coupled 'retro' with 'chic', aptly characterizing a keenness that, while looking backward, is firmly rooted in the ever-changing present. Nevertheless, Samuel's 'retrochic' occupied a broad space within popular culture, ranging from the New Age-ism of collecting crystals to historicized objects like ballpoint pens styled with Gothic fleur-de-lis designs. This book distinguishes 'retro' as a more distinct sensibility. Retro is not just a recapitulation of the past; it focuses on the recent past, even if it might seem to have slipped out of sight only yesterday.

The New Revivalism: An Unsentimental Nostalgia

One evening in August 1971, President Richard M. Nixon left behind questions of desegregating public schools, talk of visiting Mao in Communist China, criticisms of his Vietnam policy and plans for his own re-election to dine at the apartment of his newly wed daughter Tricia in New York. He then planned to see one of the most talked-about Broadway shows of the year, *No, No Nanette*, a lavish musical comedy. This revival of a 1925 hit was recommended to the president by his new son-in-law, Edward F. Cox. The president applauded frequently throughout the show, and at the end of the evening a *New York Times* reporter asked him what he thought of the stage production that had been billed 'the new 1925 musical'. The president readily endorsed the show, pronouncing himself 'in favor of nostalgia'.[14] Nixon was not alone. By the late 1960s popular press articles in *Time*, *Newsweek* and *US News and World Report* devoted considerable space to the new 'nostalgia' and its accompanying 'revivalism'. To George W. S. Trow, writing in 1974 in the *New Yorker*, the 1970s represented 'the Golden Age of Nostalgia'.[15] Quoted in an article of 1973 entitled 'Why the Craze for the "Good Old Days"', the poet Archibald MacLeish insisted that 'people are disillusioned by what's going on today, and they are returning to history for ideas about how to get out of this mess'.[16] Perhaps responding to *Nanette*'s most famous musical number, 'I Want to Be Happy', President Nixon described this feeling in simpler terms: 'after an evening like this, you go away feeling better'.[17] Writing in a *Time* magazine essay in 1971, Gerald Clarke echoed this directness, noting that 'given a choice, many Americans would put on a blindfold and pick out of a hat another year in which to live – any one of the past five hundred'.[18]

But, as Clarke quickly admitted, few Americans actually wanted to return to the fifteenth century; more to the point, the nostalgia that pervaded culture in the 1960s and early 1970s was of a distinctly modern cast, focusing on a past that had slipped away only some 20 to 100 years before. It was really the recent, modern past that people hankered after. Referring to 'the *Walton* phenomenon', a term taken from a popular television series depicting rural life in 1930s America, *US News and World Report* noted a fascination with Depression-era films, flamboyant fashions from the 1920s and 'old-time jazz'. Broadway revived not only *Nanette* but also entertained audiences with a series of shows taken from or situated in this most recent past, including the nostalgic revue *The Big Show of 1936* and Stephen Sondheim's Ziegfeld-inspired *Follies*. To some, this was indeed a 'Golden Age of Nostalgia'. But it also indicated a broader, long-term shift in attitudes towards the past. It is most ironic that, two decades after Clarke's report of widespread disillusionment with the present, the disco and bell-bottoms of the 1970s, symbols of a perceived cultural decline through much of their original incarnation, were being revived with an equal gusto.

This dissatisfaction with the present, what would soon be dubbed 'retro', cast a long shadow across the culture of the late 1960s and '70s. Yet retro is not, as Clarke and other contemporaries suggested, simply another form of nostalgia. From Charles Zwingmann to Svetlana Boym, intellectual historians have noted that the latter condition was originally conceived as a medical disease, one closely associated with homesickness. Indeed, travellers at the end of the eighteenth century feared extended journeys away from home because of the newly discovered threat of a potentially mortal illness – nostalgia. In 1710 Theodor Zwinger, a doctor and scholar based in Basel, described how Swiss mercenaries who had left their homeland to serve in the armies in France and Belgium, far from the rustic music and hearty soups of the Alps, fell ill, attempted escape and, failing that, would 'seek out death at the first opportunity'.[19] The literary historian Jean Starobinski has suggested that it was only with the advent of bacteriology and pathological anatomy in the late nineteenth century that nostalgia disappeared from medical journals, becoming the province of poets and philosophers rather than doctors.[20]

While the emotional upheaval associated with nostalgia is no longer linked with homesickness, much less deemed fatal, a bitter-sweet yearning for things, persons or situations of the past continues. Whether John Constable's painted evocations of rural Essex of the nineteenth century or Tennessee Williams's fantasized recollections of life in a small Southern town, nostalgia has had a deep influence on art and literature. Nostalgia is itself a complex emotion, often representing the past with a sadness that is blended with a small measure of pleasure. It can be private, as with Marcel Proust's madeleines. Or, as Fred Davis has suggested, it can be collective, providing a source for identity, agency or community.[21] Alfred Eisenstaedt's photo of 1945 for *Life* magazine of a sailor kissing a nurse during the Times

Square celebrations on V-J day, for example, provides a collective memory of the triumphant closing of World War Two. The nostalgia that is evoked by such images, whether private or collective, bears one point in common: it is always characterized by a certain seriousness. Nostalgia can be felt as the tug of childhood memory or as the flooding joy of relief that a difficult and prolonged struggle has been won; in either case, its associations with the past remain emphatically earnest.

If retro must be linked with nostalgia, then, to paraphrase the writer Peter de Vries, nostalgia isn't what it used to be. Where nostalgia is linked to a romantic sensibility that resonates with ideas of exile and longing, retro tempers these associations with a heavy dose of cynicism or detachment; although retro looks back to earlier periods, perhaps its most enduring quality is its ironic stance. And yet these 'retro' impulses were recognized as only half serious even as they were born. The many college students who tuned in to 'Fibber McGee and Molly', a 1930s radio programme widely broadcast again in the early 1970s, or the teenagers who filled cinemas for Bette Davis retrospectives, did so with an unsentimental smirk. Similarly, *No, No Nanette*, the 1920s musical so heartily endorsed by Nixon, was reported by Clive Barnes in the *New York Times* to resemble something like a new 'modish put-on', offering original music and lyrics but seen through 'a contemporary sensibility'.[22]

A book such as this could easily focus on evidence of the widespread and ultimate acceptance of these movements within the cultural mainstream. Instead, it traces the dynamics that led to their resurrection in the first place, examining their gradual development in the public consciousness from historical footnotes to recognition and approval within the broader culture. In limiting this study to the roots of retro, the goal is to reveal two primary points: first, to examine retro as a non-historical way of knowing the past; and second, to highlight the significance of such revivalism. Retro is a phenomenon that can be traced across a wide array of media, from television to theatre, architecture to fashion. In music alone the term has come to encompass entire genres from the post-war period, distinguishing, for instance, lush 1950s cocktail and lounge music from more serious jazz. Several tomes could be devoted to retro's many forms, bridging high and low culture. Since its rise is most extensive in the visual arts, however, this study will focus on the roots of retro as they develop in art and design. But this is also a study of retro's entry into popular culture.

Retro suggests an admiration for the past, but is also mingled with a sense of detachment that separates it from the high-minded seriousness of nineteenth-century revivalism, where the present was seen as the culmination of a progressive evolution of human knowledge. Referring to the art and design of the past helped to present contemporary achievements as the zenith of a progressive development that grew over many centuries. By contrast, retro does not look backwards in order to dignify or elevate contemporary society. Many artistic gestures in the post-war period have been suffused with a retro sensibility, whether Roy Lichtenstein's paintings and sculptures that reconfigured Art Deco's visual vocabulary, the movie-star glamour of the Art Deco 'props' used in Andy Warhol's audacious films, or the Italian neo-Liberty architects' recycling of forms from the *tempi felici* of the late nineteenth century.

In many ways, such attitudes would suggest that retro could be interchangeable with Postmodernism. Just as historians and philosophers began to question the representation of history and cultural identities, art and design began to reflect these changes. The attributes of retro, its self-reflexiveness, its ironic reinterpretation of the past, its disregard for the sort of traditional boundaries that had separated 'high' and 'low' art, all echo the themes found in Postmodern theory. In 'Nostalgia for the Present', an essay published in *Postmodernism or the Cultural Logic of Late Capitalism* (1991), the theorist Fredric Jameson saw the Postmodern condition reflected in an 'eclipse of historicity'. Describing some of the hallmarks closely associated with retro, Jameson found contemporary culture 'irredeemably historicist, in the bad sense of an omnipresent and indiscriminate appetite for dead styles and fashions', which are recycled as empty stylistic gestures.[23] This notion of recycling touches on ideas also found in Baudrillard's study of contemporary historical cinema; here, Baudrillard argues, 'history has retreated, leaving behind an indifferent nebula, traversed by currents, but emptied of references'.[24] Such critics aptly theorize a world transformed by mediated imagery and temporal rupture, suggesting stylistic forms that point to a kind of cultural amnesia. But the retro past is also implicitly linked with loss of faith in the future.

The Future That Never Was

On the morning of 22 May 1998 visitors to Disneyland, Anaheim, California discovered that the future had changed. Following a massive overhaul, the theme park whose visions of the future had titillated the world forty years earlier was at last about to reopen its famous, fanciful Tomorrowland. A throng of some 60,000 converged on Disneyland's Main Street awaiting the official 're-launch' of the park's most modern precinct. At the gateway to Tomorrowland, the tense excitement mounted as children, teenagers and adults were restrained by a crew of costumed Disney employees. When the velvet ropes finally dropped, the crowd discovered a Tomorrowland that one critic suggested 'begins with Jules Verne and ends with Buck Rogers'.[25] In short, it was a vision of the future that never was.

Disneyland's ad campaign for Tomorrowland began months in advance. Stories appeared in numerous local and national newspapers, while television programmes recapitulated its history and tempted viewers with advance peeks at this 'exciting new vision of the future'. Still, visitors entering the new Tomorrowland were confronted with a visualization of the future that was almost fifty years old. Walt Disney's original goal – to try to identify and define what the future would be – had been abandoned, a victim of technological acceleration and social unpredictability. Indeed,

Entrance to Disneyland's Tomorrowland, Anaheim, California, c. 1960.

by 1998, Tomorrowland had already been revised three times; during the 1950s Tomorrowland was initially conceived as 'the world of 1987'. But Disneyland faced an even larger problem: confronted with frightening dystopias, which more and more frequently shaped popular views of the future from the past twenty years, park officials found themselves hard pressed to present 'a future that you'd actually want to visit'.[26] In the new Tomorrowland, the future had become retro.

Retro implicitly invokes what is yet to come, as well as what has passed. The Disney designers were confronted with a problem that has suffused culture for at least the last thirty years: disentangling ideas of Modernity from contemporaneity and living in the present moment is difficult. In spite of its forward-looking 'flying saucer' bumper cars and all-plastic House of the Future, Disney's Tomorrowland was shaped by a vision that had its roots in the nineteenth century. Striving to link technology and society, aiming to create designs of the best visual and practical use, Walt Disney embraced a form of Modernism that was closely linked to industrialization and the promise to create a better world. Retro memorializes not just the Modern past, but also the utopian and optimistic ideas of these earlier eras. In the nineteenth century inventions like the photograph and telegraph convinced the public that the present was utterly different from what had come before. At their best, Modernists aimed to create a utopia based on technological change, social improvement and a methodical progress away from the past; the idea of Modernity included a relentless form of optimism, a belief that the future would inevitably become better and better. In the early twentieth century ideas like relativity theory and quantum mechanics only reinforced such thinking. Walt Disney's Tomorrowland presented a bracing vision for a progressively better and better future. Conversely, the nostalgia of Main Street USA was strictly off limits in Tomorrowland. Such Modernist values had little use for history or its turbulent flow of changing styles. The past was flawed, an unacceptable state that society was struggling to transcend.

Any study of retro inevitably focuses on the dissolution of these ideas. Retro's delinquency within the design tradition began in the years after World War Two, when Modernist ideas of futurism and 'good design' began to lose their influence. Writing in *Design* magazine in 1968, Christopher Cornford equated the hallmarks of Modernist design with 'cold rice pudding'. Both, he noted, are 'plain, nutritious, high-minded, and off-white', and both are 'monotonous'. Many began to agree with Cornford, perceiving a 'sense of malaise, misfit, of the need for new directions of thinking and new kinds of sensibility' growing in the visual arts.[27] Looking back to older periods and styles was not just nostalgic, it also suggested, as Cornford put it, 'the search for a vitamin', a kind of elixir.[28] When Clarke wrote in 1971 that 'we seem to be not so much entering the new decade as backing away from it full steam astern', he could have been speaking for a number of artists and designers, as well as the general public.[29]

But it is the recent past that retro seeks to recapitulate, focusing on the products, fashions and artistic styles produced since the Industrial Revolution, of Modernity. Retro, in fact, is dominated by technology and its most popular manifestations: its slogans are culled from syndicated television episodes and the movies of yesteryear; its anthems from second-hand records and obsolete advertising jingles; its visual vocabulary from defunct cars and household appliances. It evokes a memory of days that are not quite so distant, embodied in forms that are antiquated yet vaguely familiar.

In *The Condition of Postmodernity* (1989), the geographer David Harvey pointed to the year 1972 as signalling a 'sea-change' leading to 'the rise of postmodernist cultural forms'.[30] For many cultural commentators, intellectual currents began to shift even earlier, with the disillusionment caused by two world wars. But, combined with broader social, political and economic shifts in the late 1960s and early 1970s, it was clear that fundamental changes were occurring. The development of consumer economies on a global scale involved major shifts in the way that capitalism worked, and also held broader cultural implications. Political and social change seemed to elicit a crisis of ideology; as global boundaries began to blur, so too did a host of older certainties about history and its outcome. The nineteenth century saw a transition from historicism to Modernism, from veneration to aspiration.

But such aspiration has remained only that. Although Tomorrowland's House of the Future of 1957 showed glimmers of prescience, including plastic furniture, wall-mounted television screens, and microwave ovens, the park's sweeping vision for utopian progress has eluded us. Disney projected a future that never was. Nevertheless, the excitement of such futurism has proved hard to shake. Retro allows us to put such visions in perspective, to see the unshakable faith in Modernity as limited in historic scope. Subtly, retro reworking of the Modernist past as in Disney's new Tomorrowland helps to put the Modern in past tense.

Memorializing the Recent Past

We are a society obsessed with memory loss. Medicalized, our fears have focused popular attention on disorders such as Alzheimer's disease. Digitized, they have led to the search for increasingly secure and indestructible memory cards and computer chips. Retro, however, occurs not in the realm of technology or medicine but in popular culture, entertainment and advertising. And the memories it preserves are neither personal nor documentary. Representing neither a formal nor an academic attempt to preserve memory, retro embodies a communal memory of the recent past. To preserve it, a new kind of 'freelance' historian has developed outside the mainstream of artistic and historical thought. This dynamic and ever-changing group of artists, architects, designers and writers revisits the past not as scholars but as non-professional historians. Their memorialization of the recent past emerges not through traditional historical research but through the identification and acquisition of objects from the recent past, as well as the replication of its images and styles.

If this approach to the past is not derived from textbooks, it has drawn from both high and low culture of the recent past. The Italian Neo-Liberty architects, for instance, took their cues from the built environment in Turin, searching for a more innocent, pre-Fascist past associated with the city's Art Nouveau heritage. The pop artists Warhol and Lichtenstein were fascinated by the Art Deco world of Busby Berkeley musicals replayed on late-night television. Robert Smithson was drawn to Art Deco through the buildings in New York and his birthplace, Passaic, New Jersey, as well as scenes described in the 1920s and '30s pulp science fiction that obsessed him. Drawing from elite as well as popular elements of culture, the market-savvy promoters who fill the ranks of these latter-day resurrectionists increasingly take their cues from popular culture and entertainment.

Since in many ways this new form of revivalism defines the modern past in the popular imagination, advertising firms quickly identified retro as a uniquely attractive 'pitchman' for a sophisticated audience. Beginning with the Art Nouveau and Art Deco revivals, retro's rapid rise in the 1960s must be linked with larger developments in mass media and communications. Mass-market magazines and blockbuster museum shows flourished, and the period saw the proliferation of art and populist design 'experts' eager to break traditional confines. Hollywood increasingly produced historicizing films, for example Arthur Penn's *Bonnie and Clyde* (1966), that carefully recreated the styles and forms of the recent past but were also notably up-to-date in their content. Once adopted by filmmakers, small entrepreneurs and Madison Avenue marketers alike, retro not only became profitable, but it was also rendered intelligible.

For the art historian Thomas Crow, the avant-garde in art has served as a kind of 'research and development' branch of the popular cultural mainstream.[31] Retro offers an interpretation of history that taps nostalgia and an undercurrent of ironic understanding. Steeped in satire and humour, retro's revivalist imagery has made its way into the mainstream, shaping how the recent past is presented in advertising, film, fashion and a host of forms of popular culture. Originally intended to symbolize the dynamic changes of the Russian Revolution, geometric red-and-black forms and harsh, angular typefaces have been resurrected in order to sell cold tech music. Films like Ken Russell's *The Boy Friend* (1971) and George Lucas's *American Graffiti* (1973) present the quaint forms and mores of recent history. The retro past has become a form of public property.

For Baudrillard, retro demythologizes the past, distancing the present from the big ideas that drove the 'Modern' age. Baudrillard's perception that ours is a Postmodern age rests on the contention that we have lost touch with the 'real'. Modern cultural forms like the cinema, he argues, simulate reality. 'The great event of this period, the great trauma,' he writes, 'is this decline of strong referentials, these death pangs of the real and of the rational that open onto an age of simulation.'[32] Examining such hallmarks of 1970s cinema as *Chinatown* and *Barry Lyndon* in 'History: A Retro Scenario', Baudrillard reveals a pervasive nostalgia for the past. According to him, history 'has retreated, leaving behind it an indifferent nebula, traversed by currents, but emptied of references'.[33] For Baudrillard, retro attempts to resurrect the past 'when at least there was history'.[34] Along with the unconscious, he argues, history has become one of the few enduring myths of our age.[35] Simulating history rather than making it, retro demythologizes its subject.

From resurrections of Beardsley's drawing style to the renovated Tomorrowland, retro regards history with a jaundiced eye; its view of the past removes, rather than invests, meaning. At the beginning of the twenty-first century, it is hard to claim that retro has swept away history altogether; moreover, we can still have a sense of history at the same time as enjoying retro nostalgia. But retro has been overlooked as a crucial indicator of our time. Like the retro rockets that introduced the term into popular speech in the early 1960s, retro provides a form of deceleration or opposite thrust, forcing us to take stock of our perpetual drive to move forwards in space and time. Retro recall marks the past, however 'Modern' it styled itself, as truly past. Rather than emphasizing continuity, retro implicitly ruptures us from what came before. When we are separated from what has gone before us, retro's oppositional pull is strong.

CHAPTER ONE

When Art Nouveau Became New Again

When the British writer Evelyn Waugh visited Barcelona in 1929, the city was hosting the International Exhibition best remembered for Mies van der Rohe's glass, travertine and marble German Pavilion, which was emblematic of the Modernist movement. On his last day in the Spanish city, as Waugh wandered alone down a great boulevard, he encountered 'what I took to be part of the advertising campaign of the exhibition. On closer inspection I realized that it was a permanent building which, to my surprise, turned out to be the offices of the Turkish Consulate.' He circled the building with a camera, unable to get a proper picture because trees kept blocking his view. Instead, he hailed a cab and demanded to see more buildings by the same architect. Waugh's driver quickly acquainted him with the work of Antoni Gaudí, delivering him to Casa Milà, Park Güell and finally Sagrada Família, the massive unfinished church that the writer later called Gaudí's 'supreme achievement'.[1] Yet when Waugh's compatriot George Orwell reached Barcelona during the Spanish Civil War several years later, he made a point of visiting the Sagrada Família but pronounced it 'hideous', alleging that 'the anarchists showed bad taste in not blowing it up when they had the chance'.[2]

Waugh's and Orwell's disagreement over Gaudí's church was a clash that transcended personality. By 1929 the general public held in contempt the very qualities that helped to define what Waugh described as the 'writhing, bubbling, convoluting, convulsing soul' of Art Nouveau. Even Waugh hesitated to express too much enthusiasm for Gaudí, proclaiming that the Art Nouveau architect would be a great example 'of what Art for Art's sake can become when it is wholly untempered by considerations of tradition or good taste'.[3] Considering Art Nouveau's rapid descent in reputation in the first decades of the twentieth century, its subsequent revival in the post-war period is all the more striking.

By the 1960s the older style was not only resurrected but flourishing; represented both in museum exhibitions, such as *Art Nouveau: Art and Design at the Turn of the Century* at the Museum of Modern Art in New York in 1960, and mass-marketed wallpaper, like Cole & Son's reintroduction in 1966 of designs by the Scottish architect Charles Rennie Mackintosh. The style enriched popular and artistic icons of the 1960s, touching both the staid homemaker's monthly *McCall's* and Wes Wilson's psychedelic concert posters. The rehabilitation of Art Nouveau design, however, like the works of the British illustrator Aubrey Beardsley, was also pervaded by a retro sensibility; it contained within it an ambiguous quality, recalling Waugh's hesitant enthusiasm for Gaudí.

For many artists, curators, graphic designers and journalists, the resurrection of Art Nouveau represented emancipation from the Modernist conventions that dominated visual culture in the post-war period. The subversive aspects of Art Nouveau were represented not so much in its swirling forms or pronounced line but rather in its association with a liberating irrationality that filtered broadly into popular culture throughout the early 1960s. Sometimes dubbed 'kinky classics'[4] and 'the erotic style',[5] Art Nouveau seemed to embody social and sexual freedoms that stood in opposition to prevailing bourgeois values. The post-war recovery of Art Nouveau also played a major role in the development of Camp, both as a theoretical apparatus and as an aspect of commodity culture. Indeed, this re-use of Art Nouveau to critique later forms of Modernism was later used in one of the first instances of marketing 'cool' to a general populace. Imitation may be the sincerest form of flattery, but the Art Nouveau revival was more than creative thievery; its campy reincarnation of the 'Modern style' may have seemed new again, but Art Nouveau's claim on contemporaneity was clearly past.

The 1900 Style(s)

In its original manifestation Art Nouveau was varied, complex and widespread – qualities often overlooked in its post-war resurrection. The style appeared in Europe and America in the 1890s and reached its height at the Exposition Universelle in Paris in 1900. So far-reaching was its influence that the 'new art' encompassed such British members of the aesthetic movement as Beardsley and Charles Rennie Mackintosh, but also included representatives in Germany, where the style was known as *Jugendstil*; Italy, where it was referred to as *Stile Liberty* (or the Liberty Style); and Spain, where it was called *Modernisme*. It was in France, where Siegfried Bing founded his influential Paris shop L'Art Nouveau in 1895, that the style received its best-known name.

A truly international style, Art Nouveau expressed a variety of tendencies but generally encompassed an anxious, eclectic ornamentation based on organic motifs. Art Nouveau designers prized artifice; even three-dimensional forms were rendered in a linear, two-dimensional manner, from the whiplash curve of Henry van de Velde's squirming candelabra to Hector Guimard's stem-like columns and twisting tendrils of the Paris Métro entrances. The style stretched across Europe, however, and its impact extended beyond the sinuous linearity of Belgium, France and Germany. Thus the stylized grid of Josef Hoffmann's Palais Stoclet or the bowed rectangles of Mackintosh's and the MacDonald sisters' designs for Glasgow tearooms have also been dubbed Art Nouveau.

Even as Victor Horta designed the restless lines that run throughout the external columns, windows and balconies of the townhouse for the Belgian chemical magnate Armand Solvay, and Louis Comfort Tiffany filled the Fifth Avenue home of the sugar tycoon H. O. Havemeyer with delicate glass lamps and decorative friezes, many of the style's most memorable landmarks were created for broader segments of the urban public. Art Nouveau appealed to Glasgow's burgeoning middle classes seeking tearooms as alternatives to smoke-filled pubs, while it was embraced by the urban commuters who descended daily into the Paris Métro and adopted by Brussels workers gathering for assemblies in newly built meeting halls. Art Nouveau design also graced commercial structures and advertising materials intended to reach the urban lower and middle classes, such as Jules Chéret's frothy posters for Parisian cafés and Peter Behren's model rooms for the Wertheim Department Store in Berlin. Many of the best examples of the Art Nouveau were created for retail or widely distributed as advertisements.

If the style was impregnated with economic and social paradox, it was similarly suffused with aesthetic tensions. Most designers who worked in the style considered themselves artists and many rejected ideas of mass production in favour of traditional handicraft. But, for all the interest of Art Nouveau designers in hand-blown glass and ornately carved wood, there was an equally prevalent fascination with such modern materials as cast iron and industrial production processes like chromolithographic printing. Guimard's unprecedented green cast-iron and glass designs for the Paris Métro combined structural integrity with resplendent ornamentation; the sinuous plant-like forms twist into glittering canopies and bud-like lighting fixtures, transforming functional elements into exuberantly biomorphic forms. In Brussels, Horta's gracefully writhing banisters of wound and buckled iron echo the plant-like calligraphy in the mosaic floors and painted walls of the Solvay and Tassel houses. Although whiplash curves and delicate tendrils most inspired Art Nouveau's post-war enthusiasts, a more austere, geometric approach also came to be associated with 'the 1900 style'. Where twisting lily roots and arching drag-onflies dominated French and Belgian Art Nouveau, geometric variations could be found in the Vienna Secession and works by the Glasgow School. Mackintosh's severe linear patterns admitted references to eggs, trees and rosebuds. Secessionist designers like Hoffmann favoured rectilinear forms augmented by judicious curves, fitting floral rosettes and sprawling vines into cubes and spheres.

As new as Art Nouveau seemed in its own time, however, it bore traces of a more complex past. At the turn of the twentieth century its reflection of contemporary life was widely deemed its chief attribute; many critics and artists maintained that it resolutely rejected the past. While Art Nouveau imagery marked a deep-seated cultural shift, many of its motifs remained rooted in familiar historic styles, for instance the French Rococo or Celtic coils and interlace.

With their *psychologie nouvelle* of the 1890s, Jean-Martin Charcot and Hippolyte Bernheim hypothesized the external world's direct influence on the internal nervous system, inspiring the French Symbolist artists Gustave Moreau, Odilon Redon and Auguste Rodin to present dreams as allegory. Similarly, Art Nouveau designers like Emile Gallé employed swirling, 'nervous' lines and distorted forms to suggest complex dream-like states. Where psychologists advocated retreat into calming interiors to relieve exhausted nerves, the densely appointed interiors of Horta and vases by Gallé seemed to reflect apprehensive psychological states.[6] Art Nouveau's twisting, dripping, vegetal forms and its self-conscious evoca-tions of the human figure also insinuated a new understanding of eroticism that emerged from changing perceptions of human sexuality. Sex was first studied scientifically during the late nineteenth century, and the term 'homosexual' was coined during this period. Implicit and sometimes explicit homosexual themes abound in Beardsley's leering satyrs and wilting youths, who cavort in unusual, and often suggestive, poses. For others, this sensibility was more allusive. Androgynous figures, like the asexual lovers in Behrens's poster *The Kiss* (1898), frequently blurred distinctions between male and female.

At the turn of the twentieth century this ability to reflect the new age was deemed the style's chief attribute, leading many to call it 'the Modern style'. Its supporters claimed high status for Art Nouveau as an entirely 'new' art; Art Nouveau's claim to Modernity made it part of a new era. Nevertheless, while some critics praised this characteristic, others began to refer to the style as 'grotesque', 'unhealthy' or even 'the outcome of diseased minds'.[7]

From 'Fantastic Malady' to 'Neo-Liberty'

Even as its popular appeal peaked in the early twentieth century, Art Nouveau's critical reputation began its decline. In Britain, the style was increasingly associated with aestheticism and particularly with Oscar Wilde, who had been imprisoned for homosexuality in 1895. 'Pillory, L'Art Nouveau at South Kensington', an article published in 1901 in the *Architectural Review*, dubbed the style a 'fantastic malady'.[8] Interviewed in a *Magazine of Art* article of 1904, architect Charles Voysey identified Art Nouveau with 'a debauch of sensuous feeling', calling the style 'distinctly unhealthy and revolting'.[9] By 1930 the American historian Lewis Mumford recalled Art Nouveau as dominated by a 'meaningless stylistic exuberance'.[10] When John Betjeman surveyed the style in the same year he admitted that it had produced 'many a hideous little side table, many a sickly front door'.[11] Historians might have consigned the style to oblivion had it not been for two competing forces. A small group of scholars, many aligned with the still-young Museum of Modern Art (MoMA) in New York, attempted to rehabilitate the Art Nouveau as seminal to Modernism. Concurrently, the Spanish Surrealist artist Salvador Dalí and the architects from the Italian 'Neo Liberty' group argued for an alternative set of associations. The ensuing friction led Art Nouveau from the functionalism advocated by the German-born British scholar Nikolaus Pevsner in the 1930s to counter-cultural darling of the 1960s.

Initially, the legacy of Art Nouveau was debated within the rarefied confines of MoMA, and with its founding in 1929 the museum's first director, Alfred Barr, struggled to find 'historical precedents and antecedents that would give modern art roots and a respectable past'.[12] Barr and a small group of colleagues tried to establish Art Nouveau as a kind of doddering but significant relation to Modernism. The older style had sunk so low in scholarly esteem that he fought an uphill battle.

Nevertheless, in 1933 Barr managed to persuade the American architect Philip Johnson, a friend and founding head of the museum's department of architecture, to mount a small exhibition highlighting 'the 1900 style'. The tiny show was a marvel of cross-purposes. Johnson frankly embraced the aesthetic sanitization of the Bauhaus and was already planning the museum's ground-breaking *Machine Art* exhibition of modern industrial technology, held in 1934. He claimed that *Objects 1900 and Today*, which paired a range of Art Nouveau objects with their contemporary counterparts, compared 'two modern periods', while demonstrating that 'one is not necessarily better than the other'.[13] The exhibition, however, revealed a showdown between the generations. A contemporary Wilhelm Wagenfeld lamp, taken from Johnson's New York apartment, was juxtaposed with a bronze Art Nouveau lamp borrowed from Johnson's mother. Although Johnson ultimately abandoned the original title, *Decorative Objects from 1900 vs. Useful Objects of Today*, it reappeared as a slogan in the final show and disclosed his ambivalent embrace of Art Nouveau; the exhibition revealed his bias against a style deemed too ornamental in the era of functionalism. Praised in a *New Yorker* review as an 'adventure in smart

Installation of *Objects 1900 and Today*, 1933, Museum of Modern Art, New York.

installation . . . that tends to make the rest of the museum look rather stodgy and forlorn',[14] the chaste white interiors presaged Johnson's *Machine Art* exhibition and established him as an arbiter of taste, while instituting a museological austerity that set the Art Nouveau ornament to disadvantage.

But Barr's battle to establish the legitimacy of Art Nouveau continued, and he gradually eroded resistance to it. Art Nouveau made a brief appearance at the museum's show *Dada and Surrealist Art* (1936). In 1942 Barr pushed the museum to accept bequests from the widow of Hector Guimard, who had died in anonymous exile in New York. When the French government rejected Adeline Guimard's offer in 1948 to donate to the nation the couple's spectacular Paris townhouse at 122 avenue Mozart, Barr overrode the museum trustees and acquired still more from Guimard's estate.[15] Barr also joined forces with like-minded scholars, including Pevsner; in his treatise *Pioneers of the Modern Movement from William Morris* to *Walter Gropius* (1936), Pevsner situated Art Nouveau as a forerunner of contemporary Modernism.[16] His ideas were well received in New York, and in 1949 MoMA even reissued the book under its own prestigious imprimatur. Nevertheless, while Barr and Pevsner worked to establish Art Nouveau as a precursor to Modernism, its popular re-emergence portrayed the older style as a kind of Modernist alternative.

Indeed, just as Barr was contriving to integrate Art Nouveau into MoMA, Dalí was also noting the 'long and disgraceful repression' of the older style, but he decided to 'take revenge' in a different fashion.[17] Childhood visits to Barcelona had introduced the young artist to the melting columns, sinuous terraces and reptilian grotesqueries of Gaudí's Park Güell. Years later, Dalí maintained that the strangely molten and dreamlike forms of French and Spanish Art Nouveau echoed the Surrealists' aesthetic agenda. Although he first wrote of the style in his book *The Visible Woman* (1930), his article of 1933, 'De la beauté terrifiante et comestible de l'architecture modern style', was his most extended meditation on Art Nouveau.[18] Illustrated with photographs by Man Ray, whose eerie images transformed the Paris Métro entrances into grotesque alien heads, Dalí presented the style as fundamentally irrational. Wilfully ignoring the more restrained, studied geometries that prevailed in its Scottish and Austrian versions, Dalí praised designers like Guimard and Gaudí as representing 'the fringe of architecture'. Facing down 'the fat pigs of contemporary aesthetics, those defenders of execrable "modern art"', Dalí argued for Art Nouveau as 'something worth opposing to the whole history of art'.[19]

Not only did Dalí's contemporary paintings, such as *The Profanation of the Host* (1929), incorporate curved and undulating shapes reminiscent of Art Nouveau design, but his Surrealist objects also followed suit. Beginning in the early 1930s, he collaborated with the French designer Jean-Michel Franck in reworking several Art Nouveau chairs; replacing a leather seat with one made of chocolate, or substituting a foot with a Louis XV doorknob, he rendered them virtually useless. But his most sophisticated

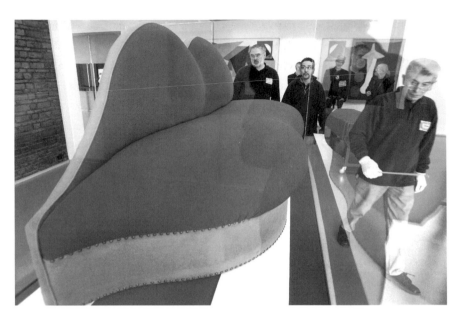

Mae West *Lips Sofa* after a design by Salvador Dalí; Boymans van Beuningen Museum, Rotterdam, 2005.

reinterpretation of the Art Nouveau style was his *Lips Sofa* of 1936–7, a piece of furniture modelled on the film actress Mae West's extravagantly bee-stung lips. In drawings like *The Birth of Paranoiac Furniture* (*c.* 1936), Dalí transfigured the star's face into a bourgeois apartment, with picture-frame eyes, a fireplace nose and a lips-shaped sofa (he later constructed the sofa with Franck's help). Mae West's characteristic feathered dresses and hourglass figure, as well as her preference for roles set in the 1890s, already associated her with the *Belle Epoque*. In his autobiographical *Secret Life of Salvador Dalí* (1942), the artist published a photo of Gaudí's Casa Milà next to the *Lips Sofa*, asserting that the building's curvaceous wrought-iron balconies resembled Mae West's mouth. But its irrationalism was also a rebuke to the prevailing International Style.

Dalí was intrigued by Art Nouveau's evocation of dream imagery, which embodied late nineteenth-century *psychologie nouvelle*. He listed 'release, freedom, development of unconscious mechanisms' among the style's 'chief attributes'.[20] For Dalí, Mae West evoked erotic desire and irrationality, suggesting aspects of the paranoiac-critical theory that he had developed in reaction to Freud. Alternatively, Art Nouveau was suffused with Freudian oral fixations; Dalí praised the works of Gaudí and Guimard as 'edible'.[21]

Mixing erotic attraction with aesthetic freedom, Dalí's recapitulation of Art Nouveau audaciously embraced the past at a time when the Modernist vanguard dedicated itself to looking forward. Disregarded by the Surrealists, Dalí's contrarian stance was adopted by others, including the Turin architect Carlo Mollino. Like Dalí, Mollino evaded the contemporary pull towards Rationalism, favoured in Italy by vanguard fascist contemporaries. Mollino's interior of the Casa Devalle (1939), designed for his friend and architect Giorgio Devalle, included Mollino's own homage to Dalí – a reinterpretation of the *Lips Sofa*.[22] Mollino shared with Dalí an interest in the Barcelona architect Gaudí; in 1949 he even designed a seat that he called 'the Gaudí Chair'. Mollino's best-known pieces, like the

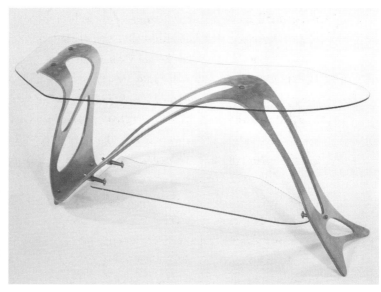

Carlo Mollino, Arabesque table, *c.* 1950, Victoria and Albert Museum, London.

Arabesque table (*c.* 1950), retain Gaudí's influence. Like Dalí, Mollino actively embraced the irrationality of Art Nouveau, believing that 'everything is permissible as long as it is fantastic'.[23]

In some ways Mollino spearheaded a broader memorialization of Italy's post-war avant-garde, recalling not so much Art Nouveau as the basis for Modernism but rather the *tempi felici* (happy times) of the late nineteenth century. Italy was not the only formerly fascist country to embrace Art Nouveau during the post-war years. Battered by Nazi claims that the style was too 'refined', 'esoteric' and 'decadent',[24] Jugendstil and the Vienna Secession emerged in the late 1940s as the darlings of European museums, resurrected and analysed with increasing seriousness by those in Frankfurt, Hamburg, Munich and Zurich. It was in Italy, however, that a loosely affiliated group of young architects and designers provided an alternative recapitulation of the late nineteenth-century style dubbed 'Neo Liberty'.

Known in Italy as the *Stile Liberty*, after the London-based department store Liberty & Co. that helped to disseminate a British interpretation of the style throughout Europe, the Italian Art Nouveau emphasized more traditional forms of ornament, especially floral decoration, than its French and Belgian equivalents; one of the style's alternative Italian monikers was the *stile floreale*. Displayed at the *Prima Esposizione d'Arte Decorativa Moderna* in Turin in 1902, the Liberty style announced Italy's arrival on the modern design scene. The country's new professionals built many Liberty houses and apartments in the north, and later generations of Italians would associate the style closely with the country's headlong sprint towards industrialization and urbanization. While most Liberty buildings were actually constructed in the leafy residential districts of Turin or Parma, in the collective imagination of post-war Italians they might as well have existed on some golden horizon, embodying the nation's early industrial aspirations and potential for future prosperity.

The Italian Art Nouveau's seductive charms were also unsullied by fascist associations. Liberty suffered during the inter-war years, as fascist critics alternately favoured rigidly rational buildings or a historicist classicism that reflected notions of ancient empire or *Romanità*. Denounced as overly ornamental or foreign, many Liberty buildings were destroyed. After Mussolini's fall, however, even Neo-Liberty's former critics understood the emotional appeal of the older period. As the Italian critic Bruno Zevi, an opponent of the Neo-Liberty architects, admitted, 'our grandfathers did less harm, even while plastering their architectural pastry with whipped cream, than our fathers and elder brothers [of the recent fascist generation]'.[25]

Italy's lingering affection for Art Nouveau expressed not only nostalgia but also functioned as a kind of symbolic code for a historically based form of dissent for the generation that followed Mollino. Never a closely defined school, the Neo-Liberty group encompassed architects, editors and journalists; to their detractors they seemed situated, as one critic put it, 'on the lunatic fringe of Italian design'.[26] Sergio Asti, Gae Aulanti, Aimaro d'Isola, Roberto Gabetti, Vittorio Gregotti, Ernesto Rogers and Aldo Rossi were all linked to Neo-Liberty at one time or another. Two of Mollino's former students, the Turin architects Gabetti and d'Isola, were among the first to immerse themselves in the local Art Nouveau tradition; in 1950 Gabetti even joined the faculty of the Turin Polytechnic, where Mollino was then teaching, to be the older architect's assistant. Their designs, like that for the Bottega d'Erasmo, a centre for Jewish studies, fused Art Nouveau with other decorative elements. The building's erratically projecting windows recall the Glasgow School of Art, while its pointed arches suggest those of a mosque. The symbolic use of Art Nouveau forms, combined with historic and geographic allusions, provided a critique of rationalism that did not go unnoticed by contemporary critics.

By recovering Art Nouveau from musty museums and incorporating its influence into new buildings, Neo-Liberty architects flabbergasted the supporters of Modernism. After their work was described in an article of 1957 in *Casabella Continuità*, Gabetti and d'Isola were branded heretics by Zevi, who saw Neo-Liberty as an 'obvious symptom' of 'human decadence'.[27]

Roberto Gabetti and
Aimaro d'Isola,
Bottega d'Erasmo,
Turin, 1953–6.

In 1959 the British critic Reyner Banham identified Neo-Liberty as an 'infantile regression'. Like his teacher Pevsner, Banham believed in Art Nouveau's historical import, but he stopped short of revisiting it. Citing the Neo-Liberty style as a 'retreat', he believed that 'to put on those old clothes again is to be, as Marinetti's words described Ruskin, "like a man who has attained full physical maturity, yet wants to sleep in his cot again, to be suckled again by his decrepit nurse, in order to regain the nonchalance of his childhood"'.[28]

Form and Reform

Across the Atlantic, Art Nouveau was similarly emerging as a statement of aesthetic disaffection. A small subculture of artists, curators and journalists adopted the style as a relief from what the contemporary scholar and critic

John Jacobus called 'our own special ennui, a dissatisfaction with too much that is implacably rational in post-1945 architecture'.[29] Others, however, complained that Art Nouveau had been embraced by 'chi-chi-ists'.

Post-war Americans did not grapple with a fascist legacy; the art and design establishment unambiguously adopted Modernism as a commodity that expressed economic affluence and cultural sophistication. Summarized in the post-war 'Good Design' movement, a Modernist approach towards product design closely associated with MoMA, it represented a calculated blend of simplicity and functionalism, mass-production and quality. The austere, unornamented furnishings highlighted in a series of MoMA-sponsored 'Good Design' exhibitions, for example, were paragons of Modernist principles, meant to reform society one middle-class home at a time. But the recovery of Art Nouveau, especially the work of the designer Louis Comfort Tiffany, in post-war America played a different role. In the 1950s journalists and collectors introduced Art Nouveau to the American public not as a positivist design reform movement, but rather with intonations of exoticism and personal liberation. Suddenly the profuse sensibility of Tiffany was rediscovered to possess a 'giddy chicness'.[30]

Whether Tiffany was chi-chi or otherwise, his reputation had been in critical freefall for several decades. His designs, often in lustrous or iridescent glass, had filled opulent interiors at the turn of the century. 'He was at the peak of chic around 1900', noted the cultural commentator Aline B. Saarinen, but he had fallen 'to the gutter of derision around 1920 to 1930'.[31] Tiffany glass diffused a whiff of moral decadence; during its decline many aesthetes treated it as a kind of 'devil's fifth column penetrating our homes'.[32] When Tiffany's firm finally went bankrupt in 1932, the remaining stock was auctioned off at a small fraction of its production costs. Some unsold objects were simply thrown out. Many others were consigned to junk dealers, who broke apart the glass pieces in the famous lamps in order to gain easy access to the more valuable bronze. As late as 1954 the dealer Steven Bruce remembered visiting one second-hand merchant whose son had hung Tiffany lamps in trees, using the delicately worked glass pieces as target practice.[33]

However, just as Tiffany's posthumous fortunes had reached their nadir with the burning of his prized estate, Laurelton Hall, in 1957, his work was swept up in a 'revival'. Part of Tiffany's resurrection could be attributed to academic and museum reconsideration of his career, which culminated in a major retrospective held at the Museum of Contemporary Crafts in New York in 1958, but even more rested with a fashion-conscious interest in this cast-off style. The Abstract Expressionist painter Theodore Stamos filled his New York studio and a country house on Long Island with Tiffany, as well as with furniture by the Belgian Art Nouveau designer Louis Majorelle. Andy Warhol, then a fashionable and influential commercial artist, prominently displayed a huge Tiffany lamp in his New York apartment along with bentwood chairs, contributing to an interior design sensibility that Calvin Tompkins would later call 'Victorian Surrealist'.[34] New York dealers catering to this milieu, for example the antique-shop owner Lillian Nassau, shifted their specializations from eighteenth- and nineteenth-century objects to Tiffany. The furniture designer Edward Wormley not only used Tiffany to furnish his own luxurious apartment but also incorporated Tiffany glass and other Art Nouveau designs into his expensive designs for Dunbar furniture. The New York boutique and restaurant Serendipity Three prominently suspended a veritable forest of Art Nouveau lamps from its ceiling, both for decoration and for sale to eager collectors. The acquisitiveness of this fashion-conscious collecting impulse did not pass unnoticed: by 1955 Aline Saarinen was separating such enthusiasts from what she called 'honest' collectors. In a *New York Times* article she announced that Tiffany, and by extension Art Nouveau, had been taken up by those who 'like what is out of favor for perversity's sake'. For Saarinen, the latter collectors were clearly 'chi-chi-ists'.[35]

Perversity apart, it took taste to collect what others deemed 'junk'. Post-war Americans were engaged in unprecedented mass-market consumer-

Abstract Expressionist Ted Stamos with his Art Nouveau collection, 1958.

ism, but Tiffany was consigned to junk dealers, from New York's decidedly unfashionable Third Avenue to rural roadside stands that sold Art Nouveau lamps and used car parts. But a fascination with the detritus of mass consumption, whether flea-market finds or street trash, was sweeping the art world in the 'Neo-Dada' works of Robert Rauschenberg. Art Nouveau's reappearance put a historical spin on such scavenger aesthetics. Describing

Serendipity Three, New York, *c.* 1960.

the resurgence of interest in Tiffany in a *New York Times* magazine article in 1958, Cynthia Kellogg noted that 'one generation's cast-offs can be the next generation's collector's items'.[36] As one Manhattan dealer explained in 1956, visitors to his collection often 'sniff "Grandmother threw that out"'.[37]

By the late 1950s this 'junk' collecting began to push the Art Nouveau revival into the popular sphere. At the centre of this trend was the unlikely figure of Edgar Kaufmann, Jr, scion of a department-store fortune and associate curator at MoMA. A former student of the architect Frank Lloyd Wright, who later designed the Fallingwater house for Kaufmann's father, the younger man came to MoMA after helping curators to organize a series of exhibitions that culminated in the museum's *Useful Objects* show in 1938. Meanwhile, Kaufmann found himself 'beguiled' by the work of Tiffany. His interest in Art Nouveau hardly came in a flash of Damascus lightning: over many years he amassed a large collection of Tiffany glass. Kaufmann made converts as well: Wormley, a neighbour in the same New York building, attributed his introduction to Tiffany to Kaufmann.

This resurrection paralleled in some ways the interest that Charles and Ray Eames, Eero Saarinen and Arne Jacobsen took in exotic, protozoic forms, introducing organic Modernism to post-war Europe and America. Like the Dalí sofa that recalled Mae West's lips, biomorphism expressed a harmonious and organic response to Modernist rationalism. New materials such as fibreglass and plastics pushed many post-war designers to adopt a more organic design vocabulary. Calling Art Nouveau style the 'Bible of mid-century' design, in 1954 the designer Ettore Sottsass noted the numerous parallels between contemporary organic Modernism and Art Nouveau.[38]

Announcing that 'after forty years of stern Modernity' the world was ready for change, Kaufmann promoted Tiffany as an aesthetic antidote; he also made visible some of the scaffolding that supported this post-war phenomenon.[39] For Kaufmann, the 'drive for liberation' gave a distinct urgency to his writing; where his programme for good design often trailed clouds of *noblesse oblige*, he described Tiffany as 'exotic' and 'beguiling' –

qualities, he argued, that 'have been banished so long from modern design'.[40] Other writers repeated these intonations of glamour and personal liberation. Noting a 'Tiffany revival' in 1955, Aline Saarinen perceived that 'the qualities of fantasy, curvilinear intricacies, ornament and natural forms . . . have been virtually "verboten" in modern design'.[41] In the popular journals *Interiors* and *House Beautiful*, Tiffany was praised for his 'exoticism', and Art Nouveau was commonly described as 'sensuous', 'exhilarating' and 'brilliant'. Tiffany-filled interiors like Serendipity 3 created an atmosphere that one of its owners described as 'a wonderland' with a 'very hot house feeling, very exotic'.[42]

Unlike the reverence that surrounded organic Modernism, one of the chief characteristics of the 1950s 'revival' of Art Nouveau was the light-hearted approach that many collectors took towards their acquisitions. In an essay of 1956 on Tiffany's renewed appeal, *Harper's* magazine contrasted Art Nouveau's 'eccentricity of subtlety' with contemporary 'good taste'. Claiming that the style was 'as hideous as it is entertaining', the magazine's anonymous writer described having recently bought 'a large lampshade decorated with birds and fruit and flowers all made of brightly colored glass that is known to my children as "the thing"', a kind of aesthetic in-joke that provoked 'uneasy laughter'.[43] Even serious scholarly studies of the style were popularly interpreted as an aesthetic lark. Writing for the *New York Times*, John Canady gave qualified approval to MoMA's exhibition of 1960, *Art Nouveau: Art and Design at the Turn of the Century*, while noting the 'legitimate laughs and pleasurable aesthetic shudders' of museum visitors.[44] Art Nouveau was accepted in a curious half-serious, half-ironic manner.

One of the most articulate supporters of Art Nouveau's 'cast-off' aesthetic was Susan Sontag, and her appreciation of the style played a major role in developing Camp; Sontag's *Partisan Review* essay of 1964, 'Notes on Camp', ignored traditional chronological and aesthetic categories, while focusing attention on Art Nouveau. Although she introduced

Camp as 'undefinable', she noted its fondness for stylization and exaggeration. An essentially content-less, depoliticized aesthetic, according to Sontag, it was a taste that favoured a form of 'daring and witty hedonism'.[45] The best example of Camp, she maintained, was Art Nouveau, 'the most typical and fully developed Camp style'.[46] Not only did Sontag include Tiffany lamps and Beardsley drawings in a list of 'random examples of items, which are part of the canon of Camp', but she quickly claimed the twisting tendrils of Guimard's Métro stations and Gaudí's densely sculpted Sagrada Família as prime models for its practice.[47]

Sontag's approach to Art Nouveau was less scholarly than that of MoMA or even Kaufmann and was rooted in the retro aesthetics of the post-war period. The American composer Ned Rorem argues that she discovered the 'chief source' for 'Notes on Camp' in the Paris apartment of Elliott Stein, an expatriate American lyricist.[48] Stein's decor included then-chic Tiffany lamps along with objects ranging from a font for holy water to pictures of muscle-men. In spite of Kaufmann's popularizing writing on Tiffany, this remained an exclusive taste; as Saarinen noted in 1955, the enthusiasm for Tiffany was the peculiar fruit of a small aesthetic vanguard and it was 'still not popular with the public'.[49] To Sontag, too, an admiration for Art Nouveau, like all Camp taste, belonged to a 'self-elected class' defined by its taste. In an otherwise democratic and egalitarian culture, this sensibility defined a new type of aristocracy for whom Camp was 'something of a private code, a badge of identity even, among small urban cliques'.

While a Tiffany collection was hardly a distinguishing factor of queerness, Sontag equated Camp, and by extension Art Nouveau, with a closeted homosexual aesthetic in the post-war era. Identifying 'an improvised self-elected class, mainly homosexuals', as 'aristocrats of taste', Sontag transformed marginalization into 'private code, a badge of identity even'.[50] Where Art Nouveau had been called 'a perverse malady' and tainted by its earlier association with homosexuality, Sontag's empowering strategy transformed Art Nouveau's 'deviance' into a quality to be sought and celebrated. Whether through seeing the films of Bette Davis or owning a Tiffany lamp, Sontag suggested that a new kind of social elite was forming, one that defined itself by appreciating or owning special objects or products.

Whether 'chi-chi-ist' or Neo-Liberty, an increasingly large number of collectors, curators and journalists saw Art Nouveau as a liberation from mainstream post-war aesthetics. Conceptions of the style as positivist design reform failed to capture the popular imagination, while new ideas of Camp provided these groups with a crucial language of critical opposition. Suggesting a complex relationship to power and its subversion, Camp revelled in marginality; Art Nouveau had become a desirable and even rebellious counterpoint to 'good taste'. If the Art Nouveau revival served as an aesthetic in-joke, it also imparted a sense of detachment and even superiority to the earlier period.

The Nouveau Market

In 1966 the call for entries for the annual exhibition of the Art Directors Club in New York was a 5-foot-long poster of a nude woman posed like an odalisque, her supine body painted in Day-Glo colours. The winding, curvilinear flowers and swirling rainbows that decorated the model's body confirmed Art Nouveau's relevance to 1960s advertising and marketing. Tom Daly's design for the poster was, in fact, an amalgam of styles. But its contemporary identification with Art Nouveau demonstrated the style's growing marketing muscle and continuing appeal to graphic designers. While Art Nouveau was honoured in museum retrospectives, simulated on stage and film sets, and sought after in exclusive auction houses, the impact of its revival was most powerfully felt in the marketplace. Cloaked in the rhetoric of liberating originality and self-expression, Art Nouveau quickly became linked to selling products.

Audrey Hepburn in front of an Art Nouveau stained-glass window. *My Fair Lady*, 1964.

As Camp taste was popularized in the early 1960s, original Art Nouveau objects found an eager market. Its Campy revival inevitably enhanced the value of works of Art Nouveau artists. Until the 1960s, the French art historian Maurice Rheims reminisced in a *Time* magazine article of 1964, 'no one except King Farouk would have thought of buying Gallé vases'.[51] However, that magazine breathlessly reported that a 6-inch Gallé vase sold in the Paris flea markets had quadrupled in price in less than a year.[52] Inevitably, cheaper fakes began to flourish. By the mid-1960s manufacturers were touting lighting fixtures that suddenly seemed 'new-again', promising that cheap plastic and paper Tiffany imitations could add a 'unique note of nostalgic charm to any room'.[53] Middle-class department stores were flooded with them.

In 1964 *Time* announced that 'the revival of Art Nouveau' had arrived.[54] In art and design circles the Modernist tradition was increasingly questioned; many artists, designers and collectors sought inspiration from other cultures or the past. Victoriana and Edwardian ephemera and antiques had already found a ready market in the post-war years, but it was Art Nouveau especially that captured the public's attention. Film and stage sets, ranging from Loudon Sainthill's popular designs for the London musical comedy *Half a Sixpence* (1963) to Cecil Beaton's lush costumes and decor for the film version of *My Fair Lady* (1964), drew their inspiration from turn-of-the-century style. As another *Time* article in 1967 noted, Art Nouveau's 'comeback' influenced everything from 'TV logos to caftan prints'.[55] Interior designers eagerly sought out Art Nouveau elements in their work, and in 1966 the venerable British wallpaper manufacturer Cole & Sons resurrected some of Mackintosh's block-printed papers. Tiffany was no exception; by 1965 the pop culture commentator Gloria Steinem noted in *Life* magazine that such Art Nouveau props had become so ubiquitous that they were being used to decorate steak houses in Times Square.[56] Few of the diners at Maxwell's Plum in New York were aware of Pevsner and the attempts of the staff of MoMA to position Tiffany and Art Nouveau within the canon of Modernism, but most of the restaurant-goers recognized its Camp cachet.

As the reputations of individual Art Nouveau artists, for instance Alphonse Mucha and Guimard, were plucked from oblivion, ordinary museum retrospectives of their careers began to resemble pop concerts. When in 1966 the Victoria and Albert Museum displayed Beardsley's drawings in a survey exhibition during the normally sleepy summer season, queues stretched out from the museum's front doors. No doubt Beardsley's prominent place in Sontag's 'Notes on Camp', published just two years earlier, fuelled popular interest in the artist, as did the police raid of a shop near the museum that was selling Beardsley prints. But, writing almost five years later, the jazz singer and culture critic George Melly recalled the art less than the crowd attending the show. He was surprised to find the show

> packed with people . . . Many were clearly art students, some were beats, others could have been pop musicians, most of them were very young, but almost all of them gave the impression of belonging to a secret society which had not yet declared its aims and intentions. I believe now . . . that I had stumbled for the first time into the presence of the emerging Underground.[57]

Now ordained subversive and Camp, Art Nouveau was quickly becoming enmeshed with the counter-culture of the mid-1960s, as fine art and graphic design intermingled with fashion and rock music. Soon after the Beardsley show opened, the Beatles released the pop album *Revolver* (1966). With its Indian instrumentals and psychologically probing themes, the record announced a new direction for pop music, while Klaus Voorman's cover art intertwined photos of the quartet with nervous line drawings that nodded to Beardsley. Indeed, Beardsley prints attracted a youthful new market and many designers adapted his style to a broader range of functions, including T-shirts, napkins, matchbooks, ties, fans and even kaleidoscopes. Others used Beardsley's imagery to sell consumer products and services, as in the London barbers Samson and Delilah.

Art Nouveau evoked the rhetoric of freedom and subversion, but it was also used in one of the first instances of marketing 'cool' to a general populace. Art Nouveau became a counter-cultural mirror of mainstream commodity culture. The Tiffany lamps that decorated Serendipity Three were unabashedly on sale. When a *Harper's* writer mocked the Tiffany lamps that filled a New York junk shop in the late 1950s, he was shocked to learn of the huge demand for such 'monstrosities', not from serious collectors, but from 'people who think they're "entertaining"'.[58] Although police confiscated Beardsley prints from reputable dealers in the summer of 1966, by September they were sold under the counter at chic London clothing boutiques like Granny Takes a Trip.

The Art Nouveau-inspired Art Directors Club poster was but one example of how mainstream marketers quickly perceived the style's potential to transform staid products and publications. With its languid and sensual line, Art Nouveau had always been heavily inflected by graphic elements, but its new counter-cultural cachet soon made it an art director's

A young woman looking at Beardsley prints, *c*. 1967.

Milton Glaser,
cover for *Holiday*
magazine, 1967.

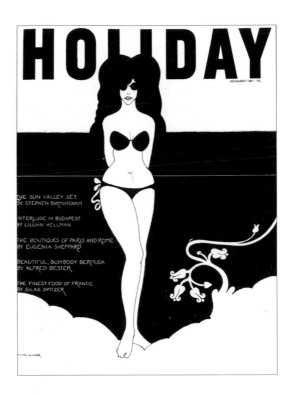

dream. Otto Storch, the art director of the venerable if stodgy women's magazine *McCall's*, gave the publication a glossily hip Art Nouveau makeover. When Milton Glaser put a Beardsely-inspired bathing beauty on the cover of *Holiday*, an aging travel magazine founded in the 1930s, it suggested consumption mingled with transgressive charm.

Whether coming from Camp, anti-Modernism or the newly emerging Underground, Art Nouveau's expressive twists, curvilinear forms and calligraphic curves provided tantalizing deviancy from accepted norms. For a generation of graphic designers for whom clarity and rationality were hallmarks of good design, as well as for typographers and illustrators who largely subordinated personal idiosyncrasies to the dictates of universal design principles, revivalist forms seemed liberating; for the designers working in this idiom, 'revival' was not a form of copying, but rather enabled self-expression. As *Print* magazine noted in 1964, it was a 'style that they feel is freer and more personal than prevalent graphic modes of the day'.[59] By 1968 Art Nouveau had even found a place in graphic design curricula. It was common for teachers to exhort their students, as an exercise of their creativity, to 'do it in art nouveau'.[60]

If the Art Nouveau revival was linked to ideas of ingenuity in some graphic design circles, by the late 1960s Madison Avenue embraced this retro-sensibility as crucial to the creation of an 'alternative' approach to marketing. Conservatism in business, and especially advertising, had dominated the industry in America after World War Two. As the 1950s progressed, however, some members of the profession criticized what was seen as self-perpetuating technocratic business practices; the competent but bland manner described in William Whyte's treatise on management, *The Organization Man* (1956), was attacked for its routine lack of creativity. Over the following decade, American business looked for new ways to enliven and transform itself. Nowhere was this more pronounced than in advertising. New ideas in demographics and the targeting of potential buyers filtered through the industry. Consumer identity and product image gained new importance. Such developments led to a 'creative explosion' throughout the advertising industry.[61]

While sophisticated data analysis set off the explosion, the industry's unprecedented embrace of counter-cultural images, slogans and music provided its popular blast. In the years following World War Two advertising design was largely dominated by sans-serif type and clear, simple layouts. However, like the city-bred Parisians who bought Rosa Bonheur's pastoral paintings of cows and colourful peasants in the nineteenth century, mid-1960s consumers gravitated towards what was fresh and unknown. The recent past was novel. From the late 1950s advertisers began to whisper a new mantra of individuality, self-expression and creativity. When Suzuki's ad campaign of 1969 urged buyers to 'Express Yourself', its marketers lived and breathed an even more seductive claim – Suzuki motorcycles had 'the power to free you'. While some designers argued that such revivals were 'sterile' exercises,[62] Art Nouveau's popular revival signalled shifting habits of consumption. Even more potent than Art Nouveau itself, by the late 1960s the revival had spawned a wanton stepchild, psychedelia, introducing an even newer visual incantation of counter-cultural magic.

Nouveau Frisco

In the spring of 1967 *Time* magazine announced that, 'like a butterfly bombarded by gamma rays, Art Nouveau is mutating, intermarrying with the eye-jarring color schemes of Op and the gaudy commercialism of Pop'.[63] Equating this mutant style with San Francisco's Haight-Ashbury district that had recently been profiled in the magazine, *Time* dubbed the new look 'Nouveau Frisco'.[64] Symbolic of a younger generation, this new Art Nouveau-inspired style was sited in a 'psychedelic dreamland' between San Francisco and Madison Avenue; if psychedelia struck the readers of *Time* as a strange mutation, it was quickly adopted by the young and not-so-young as a mainstream decorative style. Moreover, its exuberant mixing of Art Nouveau with other influences suggested that beyond recapitulating older styles, retro's rupture from the modern past could generate new hybrid forms.

Already a capital of the 1950s Beat scene, San Francisco in the mid-1960s was home to a host of counter-cultural groups, including the politically radical Diggers and the anarchically bohemian hippies, as well as to a mushrooming new music scene that attracted international attention. Bands like Jefferson Airplane and Quicksilver Messenger Service embraced 'psychedelic' performances pioneered by Ken Kesey's Merry Pranksters and the Velvet Underground, imitating the effects of drugs like

LSD through strobe lights and coloured liquid light projections. Held at such venues as the Fillmore Auditorium and the Avalon Ballroom, these events, deeply rooted in the San Francisco counter-culture, were furtively publicized on handbills and posters distributed around the Bay Area, especially near college campuses.

The posters served a double function, as community-building emblems and as expressions of the music; they also helped to initiate a psychedelic style. After being superseded in mid-twentieth-century America by television and radio, posters themselves were undergoing a revival among the young, and this revived *fin-de-siècle* advertising form in turn alluded to a new style. In an *Art International* report on San Francisco in 1967, Carl Belz noted the affinities of psychedelic posters to Pop and Op art, but he insisted that if this new poster style 'can be grouped under a single stylistic label, it would probably be Neo-Art Nouveau'.[65] That the counter-culture had already cast a moist, nostalgic eye backwards was apparent in the cast-off Edwardian frock coats and stove-pipe hats prevalent in Haight-Ashbury. San Francisco's 'postermania', meanwhile, echoed the 'poster craze' of the 1890s.

In this historicizing climate, modern psychedelia found its muse in Art Nouveau graphic design; one of the principal sources was Herschel Chipp's catalogue for *Jugendstil and Expressionism in German Posters*, a survey of *fin-de-siècle* posters held at the University Art Museum, Berkeley, in 1965. Supported by the founding director Peter Selz, the former MoMA curator who spearheaded the ground-breaking Art Nouveau retrospective of 1960, the exhibition was exactly the kind of scholarly re-evaluation of the older style that the museum had been promoting for years. Its eventual influence, however, was decidedly less predictable.

Robert (Wes) Wesley Wilson, identified by *Time* in 1967 as the 'foremost practitioner' of the psychedelic style, never saw the Berkeley exhibition; he discovered Chipp's well-illustrated catalogue in early 1966.[66] Casting around for historic poster styles, the former philosophy student was deeply

Robert (Wes) Wesley Wilson and psychedelic posters, c. 1978.

impressed by the book's flavourful Jugendstil and Expressionist imagery, and he immediately adapted what he called 'Viennese Secessionist lettering'.[67] In his advertisement of 1966 for a performance by Jefferson Airplane, Wilson imitated the cramped, decorative typography of Alfred Roller, whose advertisements for the fourteenth and sixteenth Secessionist exhibitions were reproduced in the catalogue. Wilson continued to use similar fonts in his work, and he expanded his imagery to include that of other major late nineteenth-century artists, including Mucha, Gustave Klimt and Egon Schiele.[68]

While designers quickly cribbed Wilson's hypnotic style, others scrambled to find still more examples of Art Nouveau design; after scouring the main branch of the San Francisco Public Library for Art Nouveau images, Alton Kelley and Stanley Mouse began to borrow almost verbatim from Mucha's designs. Their poster of 1966 for a performance at the Avalon Ballroom, for instance, repeats Mucha's famous advertisement of 1897 for Job cigarettes with little alteration. The poster artist Rick Griffin called the late nineteenth-century book illustrations of Gustave Doré a major inspiration.[69] Filled with tendrils of droopy hothouse plants, hovering swans and floating, languid women with tangles of coiling hair, his posters borrowed much from Art Nouveau imagery. Echoing the emphasis of Art Nouveau designers on the *Gesamtkunstwerk*, or total work of art, early psychedelic designs mixed music with art, dance with environment, giving a dream-like, LSD-induced nod to Surrealism, while echoing 'the new psychology' of the older period.

Campy in its allusions, psychedelia wagged a pot-scented finger at its Art Nouveau sources. Kelley's and Mouse's copy after Mucha, after all, pointedly included a model dangling a lit cigarette in knowing reference to the current drug culture. One of the largest poster distributors of the period called itself 'Tea Lautrec', referring simultaneously to Henri Toulouse-Lautrec, the artist often affiliated with Art Nouveau, and also to slang for marijuana. For the psychedelic artists, Art Nouveau offered a model for freedom, irrationality and emotion that recalled Dalí and Kaufmann more than Barr and Pevsner. When Wilson imitated the Viennese graphic designers, it was not for their Modernist tendencies, but rather because he admired 'the Expressionist idea of really putting it out there'.[70]

In order to play on the Elysian Fields of Golden Gate Park, Art Nouveau had been transformed into something quite different from the artistic style profiled by Chipp and represented in MoMA's scholarly exhibitions. As *Time* magazine noted in 1967 when describing San Francisco's psychedelic scene, 'in the decade since the turn-of the-century's sinuous Art Nouveau style first began to stage a comeback . . . the variations have grown increasingly bizarre'.[71] This was not a true Art Nouveau revival, but rather a kind of cross-pollination, blending with the hard-edged geometric designs of Op or Optical art, a new colour palette and motifs that drew from India and the Middle East, the visionary imagery of Dalí, René Magritte and other Surrealists, and iconography from popular culture, including comic-book iconography and familiar advertising 'personalities' such as Planters' 'Mr Peanut' and Borden's 'Elsie the Cow'.

This engagement with popular culture, though, also suggests an element of dysfunction in the counter-cultural music scene's love affair with psychedelia and – by extension – the Art Nouveau. Many of the San Francisco artists claimed that their posters were art, not business. True to the mercantile impulses of the original Art Nouveau style, however, their backward glance was frequently inflected with commercial purpose; San Francisco's poster art patrons were not Medici but rather concert promoters. Although their undulating, Art Nouveau-inspired type demanded readers' attention and helped to define an 'in-group' willing to invest time deciphering them, these posters remained primarily marketing devices. Nouveau-inspired whirls and tendrils, rendered in eye-jarring colours, soon decorated San Francisco store fronts eager to announce their counter-cultural ties.

The Bay Area rumour mill continued to suggest that local poster artists would soon be exhibiting in major New York and Los Angeles art galleries, but the San Francisco artists generally developed little traction outside the city; their Art Nouveau motifs were too easy to emulate. When Wilson took his portfolio to New York, he quickly saw that his style had been co-opted by the more upbeat and commercial imagery of Peter Max.[72] Max's ubiquitous 'Cosmic '60s' style fused Art Nouveau's sinuous and bulbous organic forms with vivid colours and photomontage techniques. They also hinted at psychedelia's exclusive in-group aesthetics but were more legible and commercially palatable than the San Francisco posters. In Britain psychedelia found an early home at the Granny Takes a Trip boutique; the shop owner Michael English joined Nigel Waymouth to form a band and also design posters as Hapshash and the Coloured Coat, blending the imagery of Mucha and Beardsley with ads for club performances and other musical happenings.

For a brief moment, the psychedelic style was a genuine evocation of the 1960s youth culture, but trendsetters quickly exploited it as a

Two hippies in San Francisco's Haight district, looking at a psychedelia-inspired store window, 1967.

marketable fashion. When John Lennon commissioned the Dutch art collective The Fool to decorate his Rolls-Royce, it was clear that the 'psychedelic cultural revolution' was changing. Tendrilled flowers, vivacious scrolls and bulging, organic shapes would be welcomed into middle-class homes in the guise of wallpaper, clothing, jewellery and furniture. Although psychedelia's root lay with the Underground, a perceived reaction to the commercialism of popular culture, its aesthetic was quickly subsumed. Again, an article of 1967 in *Time* magazine noted:

> a naked woman, body-painted like a Tiffany lamp shade, decorates the latest ads for Casino Royale; dust jackets for *Madame Sarah* and Louis Auchincloss's *Tales of Manhattan* look like so much leftover [*sic*] Alphonse Mucha. From coast to coast, be-ins, folk-rock festivals, art galleries and department-store sales are now advertised in posters and layouts done in a style that is beginning to be called Nouveau Frisco.[73]

Inspiring a generation of 'groovy ads', these newly psychedelic products served to line wallets more than expand consciousness.

Nevertheless, psychedelia's twisted take on Art Nouveau attracted mainstream advertisers, who grabbed at the fad with a kind of uneasy, purblind instinct. Just as Art Nouveau imagery, with its visual vocabulary of freedom, was a marketer's dream, members of advertising's creative revolution jumped at psychedelia's selling potential. For most, the swirling, fluorescent graphics of psychedelia provided just the kind of fairy dust necessary to perk up sales. Peter Max, whose colourful designs were soon widely imitated, appeared on the cover of *Life* magazine in September 1969 under the heading 'Portrait of the Artist as a Very Rich Man'. Ad campaigns for soft drinks and shampoo, TV sitcoms and new cars used the distended lettering and wildly contorted forms of a transformed Art Nouveau to convey the raw exuberance of the psychedelic look. Designers, such as John Alcorn, used the new style to associate a joyous insolence and good-hearted swagger with products like Eve cigarettes and Pepsi Cola. But when the commercial firm Photolettering Inc. issued a catalogue of Psychedelitype typefaces in 1969, many designers claimed that the revival was over – now anyone could set the once unreadable type.

If Art Nouveau was considered a malady at the beginning of the twentieth century, by 1970 the popular mainstream had been effectively 'inoculated'. By this time, connoisseurs of subversion had abandoned the style; Art Nouveau and psychedelia ended up on supermarket shelves and television. For late 1960s trendsetters, Art Nouveau's eventual failing was its very success; when Art Nouveau-inspired swirls embellished soft drink ads, the revival, diluted in meaning and debased in use, was dead. Scholars, auction houses and antique collectors confirmed the now-established stature of Art Nouveau as a modern style that had slipped into history. But, as it was gradually accommodated into the art historical canon, it had been replaced in the hipster's view with a more up-to-the-minute style from the modern past – Art Deco. A new Art Nouveau had been discovered.

Cover of *Life* magazine featuring Peter Max, 5 September 1969.

CHAPTER TWO

Moderne Times

In the spring of 1967, the editors at *Arts* magazine in New York and Salvador Dalí agreed that Roy Lichtenstein represented a modern Aubrey Beardsley. Ten years earlier, any comparison to Beardsley would have been unthinkable: the once-prominent leader of the Art Nouveau style had long lapsed into obscurity. In 1966, however, the Beardsley retrospective mounted by the Victoria and Albert Museum in London had reintroduced the illustrator as a provocative contemporary figure. With his aquiline face and attenuated hands, Beardsley appeared lordly and distant in the *Arts* photograph; the caption described him as 'Looking toward the future'. Opposite the photo on the facing page Lichtenstein assumed an identical pose, and the Pop Art painter seemed to be staring down the Art Nouveau draughtsman. The Lichtenstein caption read: 'Looking toward the past', and both photos accompanied Dalí's essay 'How an Elvis Presley Becomes a Roy Lichtenstein'. While scarcely mentioning Elvis in the article, Dalí instead proposed a relationship between Lichtenstein and Art Nouveau, and particularly the work of Beardsley.[1] Lichtenstein himself had earlier compared the arabesque waves in his *Drowning Girl* (1963) with the Art

Nouveau aesthetic.[2] Nevertheless, Dalí's article dismayed Lichtenstein, who maintained that he had assumed his striking pose unaware of the earlier Beardsley photograph. But Dalí and the editors at *Arts* would ultimately be vindicated. Lichtenstein, along with many of his fellow Pop artists of the mid-1960s, was already looking to the past, seeking the roots of consumer culture. Yet the real style that captured his imagination was not the increasingly popular Art Nouveau, but rather Art Deco.

The Art Deco style was born not in the 1930s but in the 1960s. Along with space-age plastics, Day-Glo colours and lava lamps, Art Deco emerged as a wildly popular phenomenon throughout Britain, Europe and the United States; by 1968 it was loosely associated with a disparate range of popular art and design movements from the inter-war years. Although critics readily applied the Art Deco label to such newly rediscovered artefacts as jazzy cigarette cases decorated with sun and cloud motifs and the sleek signage embedded in the walls of the Rockefeller Center in New York, actual definitions of the style remained fluidly ambiguous. Recognizing the half-reverent and half-ironic tone of this revival, many observers connected the style's original version with the gimmicky glamour of Pop Art.

If its visual vocabulary had become ubiquitous by the end of the decade, the term Art Deco suggested the kitschy effervescence of the late 1960s. Until then, inter-war art and design had acquired a variety of usually disparaging monikers, including 'Jazz Modern' and 'Aztec Airways'. Attempts to connect popular art of the 1920s and '30s with Modernism led to a cluster of other names, including the French *Moderne*, the English 'Modern style' and the derogatory 'Modernistic'. Many French commentators associated these design developments with the Exposition Internationale des Arts Décoratifs et Industriels Modernes, held in Paris in 1925, by referring to the entire period as 'Paris 25', 'Style 1925' or even 'La Mode 1925'. Not until 1966, when the Musée des Arts Décoratifs in Paris mounted a sweeping survey of the age, did the truncated, Pop-inspired 'Art Deco' appear as a subtitle to the museum's exhibition *Les Années 25*. Those who embraced the style, as well as those who were confounded by its sudden resurgence, quickly adopted this jocular designation.

Many strategies of consumption and marketing highlighted in Pop Art had their roots in the inter-war years. While critics frequently dismissed the Deco revival as a passing fad, the 1930s intrigued luminaries like Lichtenstein and Andy Warhol. Repeatedly plundered and popularized by decidedly non-professional historians, Deco, like Art Nouveau, was not only widely disseminated, but also freely mixed and merged in an exuberant jumble of history and metaphor. Deeply rooted in 1960s sensibilities, the impact of the newly revived Art Deco outlasted disposable paper dresses, black lights and dancing the frug; the invention of 'Art Deco' also marked the maturing of retro into a significant and persisting phenomenon. But it also marked growing ambivalence towards the machine age.

Modern Meets *Moderne*

From the glistening stainless steel embellishing the Chrysler Building in New York to chrome side tables by Eileen Gray, the style that would become known as Art Deco emerged during the inter-war years. Emphasizing new, machine-age materials and sleek or stylized geometric forms, the popular *Moderne*, or popular Modernism, was influenced by functionalist-inspired design, but lacked its theoretical sophistication. Architects and designers of the Bauhaus, de Stijl and Constructivist schools aspired to a machine-inspired functionalism as a means of social transformation. Their geometric forms and streamlined simplification consciously voided all references to the past; *Moderne* architects and designers, by contrast, favoured a form of 'modernized' classicism or 'stripped' historicism. While many Modernists condemned historicism, 'Modernistic' architects and designers frequently quoted motifs drawn from ancient

Greek, Egyptian and Aztec art. Essentially a synthesizing style, the Modernistic shared with Modernism a chrome-plated vision of the machine age, and both modes adopted a positivist attitude towards the future.

However typical of their period these two inter-war styles may seem today, they hardly dominated their age. The era was characterized by a series of revivals, including Georgian in Britain and Colonial in America. In his satiric survey *Pillar to Post: English Architecture without Tears* (1938), the British critic Osbert Lancaster caricatured *Moderne* as well as Modernism, but also paraded before his readers a bevy of now-forgotten styles popular at the time. Lancaster bestowed on them satiric names like 'Curzon Street Baroque', in reference to a 1920s vogue for grandiose Franco-Germanic influences, for example, and 'Stockbroker Tudor' to describe a reinvention of the Elizabethan houses then gaining popularity in British and American suburbs.

Like these styles, *Moderne* maintained its roots in older forms, but the trends that would become Art Deco also drew on such diverse Modern sources as the angular Wiener Werkstätte designs of Koloman Moser and Josef Hoffmann, the blunt geometry of Russian Constructivism and the fractured planes of Cubism. Sumptuously crafted and exalting in both exotic as well as more common materials, the style embodied hard-edged opulence, bristling with the kaleidoscopic motion and glossy luxury peculiar to chrome and tinted glass. Although aspects of Deco had flourished for at least a decade before the Paris Exposition of 1925, the French exhibition was crucial to its promotion and dissemination. Paradoxically, however, the elegant style announced in 1925 is only partly related to the style that emerged in the 1960s; much of what was known as 'Art Deco' was designed later, under very different conditions, in the United States and Britain.

A later, more popular phase of Art Deco brashly gloried in machine-age motifs and overshadowed the style's earlier origins; these subsequent developments also propelled the style's 1960s resurrection. The elegant though haltingly enunciated confidence in the machine age was more forcefully stated in later constructions of the Art Deco style by American designers like William Teague and Norman Bel Geddes. Moreover, economics of the Depression era mingled Modernistic aesthetics with marketing innovations. Corporations employing 'planned obsolescence' introduced fashion cycles to manufactured products, encouraging additional sales of cars or refrigerators by abruptly rendering the previous one stylistically obsolete. Streamlining, the dominant style of this later phase of Art Deco, suggested the resonant power of the machine age. The ubiquitous teardrop shape of streamlined objects represented the triumph of style as marketing strategy: Raymond Loewy's sleekly aerodynamic pencil sharpener (1933) looked poised for flight. The polished surface of Chrysler's Airflow sedan (1934) invested the car body with the look of dynamism.

Speed and technological innovation haunted the age, providing aesthetic dazzle while creating a mass culture. Radio, for instance, not only made national celebrities of Will Rogers and Rudy Vallee, but also grew into a crucial advertising medium. From bath salts to Buicks, products promoted via radio foreshadowed marketing campaigns of the post-war television era. The increasing ubiquity of Hollywood cinema, especially in the 1930s, introduced a shared visual culture of gangster films like *Little Caesar* (1931), musicals like *42nd Street* (1933) and historical dramas such as *Mary of Scotland* (1936). Whether embodied by a General Motors car or an RKO film, popular Modernism in many ways anticipated Pop.

The frankly commercial nature of popular Modernism ironically led to the style's eventual eclipse. Never embraced by serious critics, Modernistic design fell out of favour during World War Two. Modernist architects and theorists such as Mies van der Rohe and Le Corbusier had always insisted that theirs was the only legitimate claim to contemporary machine-age imagery.

Moderne was not marginalized in the post-war period; it was merely erased. Writing in 1958 in the introduction to the Museum of Modern Art's

Twentieth Century Design catalogue, the architecture curator Arthur Drexler dismissed skyscraper-shaped bookcases and other icons of Modernistic design as 'sincere but unfortunate' efforts that were simply not 'eligible for inclusion' in the museum's collections.[3] The Swiss architectural historian Sigfried Giedion introduced *A Decade of New Architecture* (1951) by asserting that Chicago's innovatory buildings of the late nineteenth century were followed by a period of almost complete disintegration. 'Far worse', he argued, than the Americans falling 'passively asleep during the first decades of the century' was the tragedy that 'during the crucial '20s Modern architecture was completely banished from the American scene'.[4] If the 'Modernistic' style did not warrant academic praise, however, it was not entirely forgotten. Social changes and shifting aesthetic criteria would force a re-examination of the 'Modernistic', heralding its late 1960s reintroduction as 'Art Deco'.

The New Art Nouveau

Long before scholars recognized it, the public was primed for a resurrection of inter-war style, if only because the heavily marketed Art Nouveau revival was rapidly losing its exclusive cachet. In a *Life* magazine article of 1965 on Camp, Gloria Steinem remarked that Tiffany lamps, previously one of the crucial markers for chic taste, ceased being a marker of in-group exclusiveness when they were used to decorate a popular New York steak house.[5] The popularity and profitability of the 1960s Art Nouveau revival made it ubiquitous in popular culture. As its popularity increased, however, its Campy exclusiveness necessarily declined, leaving adherents hungry for a newer retro phenomenon. Marketers and collectors alike cast about for a replacement, looking for the new Art Nouveau.

Many popular observers predicted the eventual vogue of inter-war design. In 1966 Hilary Gelson reported in the London *Times* that Martin

Battersby, an interior and stage designer who had only recently been one of the 'leaders of the recent art nouveau movement', had switched collecting allegiance.[6] Even Edgar Kaufmann, a major influence on the rehabilitation of Tiffany's Art Nouveau reputation, noted a shift in tastes. While reviewing a group of late 1960s Art Deco books in the *Art Bulletin*, Kaufmann rather grudgingly observed that 'the Arts [*sic*] Deco' seemed to have 'replaced Art Nouveau in the hearts of the young'.[7]

For critics in the 1960s, popular interest in the Art Deco style seemed not only logical but even inexorable. By 1971 Christopher Neve, writing in *Country Life*, granted that an Art Deco revival was only to be expected. 'The preceding preoccupation had been Art Nouveau', he intoned, 'and what could be more logical after a cursory look at the Secession and Bauhaus styles than a wild excursion into their stylistic progeny, the fizzing cocktail of influences that Aldous Huxley labelled Entre Deux Guerres'.[8] That same year, Jean Progner argued in 'Art Deco: Anatomy of a Revival' that this change represented a natural succession. 'Having happened once', Progner maintained, 'it was logical that it should happen again; the simpler, more dynamic styles of the twenties and thirties succeed in popularity the weighty and languorous intricacies that characterize Art Nouveau'.[9] Bevis Hillier leaned toward a similar stylistic argument, emphasizing that 'it did not require a Nostradamus to predict that the Art Nouveau revival would be followed by a twenties and thirties revival – history repeating itself by the superseding of a complex curvilinear style by a classically rectilinear one'.[10] As inevitably, Natalie Gittelson gushed in *Harper's Bazaar*, 'as the night follows the day, Art Deco would follow Art Nouveau as the collecting craze . . . of the great, greedy, copycat public'.[11]

If, as Janet Malcolm of the *New Yorker* reasoned in 1971, 'Art Deco changed almost overnight from an embarrassment into a historical style',[12] its rediscovery was not merely a question of winning over the young at heart. Even more than the Art Nouveau revival, Art Deco was discovered not by historians, but rather by a diverse group of retro popularizers who included writers and curators and especially Pop artists; defining and memorializing the styles and icons of their formative years, namely popular Modernism and the mass culture of the inter-war period, these artists helped to shape Art Deco into a Pop image.

Pop Went the World's Fair

The New York World's Fair of 1964–5, with its theme of 'Man in a Shrinking Globe in an Expanding Universe', would seem an unlikely location for the rediscovery of Art Deco. Symbolized by the Trylon, a 700-foot triangular tower, and the Perisphere, a fourteen-storey, 900,000-pound steel globe depicting the earth's continents spread over an orb of lattice, the event was intended to display the upcoming Space Age; one of the most popular attractions was a 'Magic Skyway' that scooted fairgoers in automatically operated Ford convertibles through a prehistoric fantasy of dinosaurs and cavemen before culminating in a gleaming, futuristic 'City of Tomorrow'.

Yet in spite of these futuristic fantasies, the event was haunted by ghosts from the past. The 1964 fair was held in the same Flushing Meadow Park as its giant predecessor, the World's Fair of 1939–40. Both events were organized by the celebrated urban planner Robert Moses and even shared some of the same buildings. Westinghouse, General Motors and other major corporations who helped sponsor the 1939–40 fair returned; General Motors updated its popular Futurama display. Westinghouse exhibited a model of a time capsule buried at the end of the 1939–40 fair along with photographs documenting space exploration and nuclear physics.

The 'Design for Tomorrow' theme of the fair of 1939–40 underscored technological and consumer advances, conveying a sense of expansive progress. The earlier fair also represented the swan song of Art Deco's influence on popular advertising and marketing; many visitors to the fair

Sculpture, fountains and Unisphere at the World's Fair of 1964 in New York.

of 1964 found themselves intrigued by the now-antique relics from the first fair. Pop artists, too, began to define and memorialize the styles and icons of their formative years, namely popular Modernism and the mass culture from the Depression. Events like the World's Fair of 1964 helped many to encounter inter-war style not through books but through the lived environment.

The exuberant, even brash consumerism of the World's Fair of 1964 mirrored contemporary popular culture. While enormous crowds lined up to see Michelangelo's *Pietà* at the Vatican pavilion, fair organizers found a kindred spirit in the nascent Pop Art movement. The US Rubber Company, for example, sponsored an 80-foot-high Ferris wheel that resembled a giant tyre; the State of Florida's pavilion was topped by a 15-foot model of an orange. New York State's pavilion, designed by Philip Johnson and Richard Foster, featured a series of murals by Pop's rising stars, including Robert Indiana, Robert Rauschenberg and James Rosenquist, along with Lichtenstein and Warhol. For many in the Pop movement, the fair's recapitulation of its predecessor underlined a nostalgic strain within Pop. Warhol, for instance, began collecting Art Deco objects around this time and would eventually amass a significant collection of 1939–40 World's Fair memorabilia. Conversely, Lichtenstein represented images from both fairs in subsequent work; *This Must Be the Place* (1965) conjured some of the second fair's principal monuments, including the Vatican Pavilion's curved wall and the slender, architectonic pylons surmounting the major exhibits, within a flattened cityscape that evoked 1930s science-fiction cartoons. Lichtenstein's work would soon become suffused with a 1930s design vocabulary, and he continued to obsess over the fair's positivist vision of consumption and nostalgia.

Beyond Pop, the World's Fair of 1964–5 also precipitated a surge of interest in inter-war art and architecture. The earlier fair's signature monuments, Wallace Harrison's Trylon and Perisphere, were rediscovered along with extant Deco landmarks. The Empire State Building, for example, received renewed attention when the skyscraper's top 30 floors were illuminated each night beginning in April 1964 in recognition of the World's Fair. This revival of its original night-time lighting design established the structure as a night-time landmark, triggering a series of magazine and newspaper articles.

The brazen enthusiasm of Deco culture also percolated into public consciousness through early 1960s film culture. Increasingly, foreign and Depression-era films found new audiences, both in newly established cinemas, as well as mainstream television broadcasting, where they provided cut-rate programming for independent stations. By the early 1960s even the major networks were dotted with 'late night shows', 'late, late shows' and 'early shows'; more than 100 inter-war films aired weekly in the New York City area.[13] New movies set in the older period, including *Some Like It Hot* (1959), *King of the Roaring 20s: The Story of Arnold Rothstein* (1961), *The George Raft Story* (1961), as well as popular television series like *The Untouchables* (1959–63), also highlighted the older period. From World's

Fair ashtrays to Busby Berkeley musicals, popular culture from the 1920s and '30s was rapidly catching the attention of mid-1960s trendsetters.

It was hardly a coincidence that Pop artists like Warhol and Lichtenstein, whose work had been prominently featured at the World's Fair of 1964–5, helped to lead the revival. Unlike the Colonial revival or Stockbroker Tudor, Art Deco's aggressive commercialism was uniquely suited for a Pop revival. From 1920s promotions by the Parisian department stores Le Bon Marché and Printemps to the triumph of streamlined planned obsolescence, Deco style dictated the patterns of consumption often highlighted in Pop Art. Advertising strategies of sloganeering and branding, perfected in the years leading up to World War Two, were quickly assimilated by Pop artists. Moreover, films, radio and comics of the inter-war years now seemed like quaint prototypes for the technological sophistication of colour television and interstellar travel. As the British critic Lawrence Alloway observed at the time, 'the machine aesthetic was anti-handcraft and anti-nature, values which are, broadly, associated with Pop art. Hence, the industrial content of Pop art has a precursor, all ironies aside, in the thirties'.[14] Hillier, in his *Art Deco* of 1968, stated that 'Art Deco has been an important influence on the most significant recent movement – Pop Art'.[15] Malcolm, however, came closer to the truth when she argued in her *New Yorker* article, in response to Hillier, that in fact 'it is the other way around. Art Deco as such (the term was coined in the sixties) would not exist if Pop Art did not exist . . . Pop Art's benign vision of mass culture is the matrix of the Art Deco revival'.[16]

Malcolm's insistence that Art Deco had been made in Pop's image reflected the older style's ahistorical nature. Much of what emerged in the late 1960s as Art Deco bore only passing resemblance to the high-quality French wares displayed in 1925; the transformation of the original French exhibition's bulky title from Exposition Internationale des Arts Décoratifs et Industriels Modernes to the slangy Art Deco epithet encapsulates the irreverent nature of the style's revival. In anointing the Art Deco as the true expression of popular design in the inter-war years, independent historians ignored a bevy of popular design styles from the period; the American Colonial and Georgian revivals, for instance, were never assimilated into what would become the Art Deco design vocabulary. Instead the Modernistic Art Deco, with its streamlined blend of technology and populism, would soon be considered the primary expression of mainstream inter-war art, architecture and design. For Pop artists, carefully selected images from this period provided a readily accessible history, an iconography for the machine age but also of a fundamentally optimistic commodity culture unsullied by economic depression and totalitarian politics.

More Modern Than We Feel Now

Roy Lichtenstein's painting of 1968, *Preparedness*, describes an austere mechanical landscape of smokestacks, pistons and cannons, an industrial scene that is both heroic and faintly ridiculous. Part factory, part laboratory, part garrison, its mechanized precision and brawny valour suggest a world designed with T-square and compass. In 1928 the 10 by 20-foot triptych might have imparted the history of aviation in a bank lobby or touted the ideal factory in a post office interior. Instead, *Preparedness* lampoons the *naïveté* behind the twentieth century's technological exuberance; the characteristic Benday dots and heavy outlines obliquely criticize American military, industrial and social misadventures from South Central Los Angeles to South-East Asia. But Lichtenstein also casts a long glance at the past, evoking notions of faith, confidence and progress through Art Deco's stylized geometric forms. As he explained at the time, 'I think that they were much more modern than we feel now.'[17]

Lichtenstein's fascination with history was not shared by the first wave of Pop artists. Richard Hamilton's happy housewives grasping Hoover

Roy Lichtenstein, *Preparedness*, 1968, Solomon R. Guggenheim Museum, New York.

vacuum cleaners were as contemporary as they were politically charged. To a later generation of Pop artists, however, Art Deco was creative catnip. The London-based artist Joe Tilson's image of the *Empire State Building* (1967) presented the 1930s landmark as if taken from a roll of film stock; his plumbing of Deco decorative forms like the ziggurat (evocatively dubbed Zikkurat by the artist) recalled Manhattan's skyline as much as Middle Eastern towers. Colin Self's *Cinema* drawings (*c.* 1964–5) exaggerated the luxurious alienation of elegantly clad women posed in streamlined interiors. Believing that he had found an inexhaustible subject, the New York artist Claes Oldenburg referenced Carl Breer's Chrysler Airflow design of 1934 for his own *Airflow* (1964–9), a sprawling project that included soft sculptures and moulded prints detailing the car's streamlined form.

While many Pop artists worked extensively with Deco motifs, the style also suggested a faded glamour, presenting themes of consumption, progress and Modernity in a new light. Memorializing the era as much through their collecting patterns as through stylistic references in their art, the leading American Pop artists Lichtenstein and Warhol viewed the era with a combination of nostalgia and irony. An early collector of Art Deco, Warhol extended his obsession with consumerism to an interest in mass media and popular culture of the inter-war years, from Borden's Elsie the Cow to Fred Astaire and Ginger Rogers musicals. Lichtenstein, too, collected Art Deco pieces during this period. But mechanical landscapes like *Preparedness* represented an era that he found both intriguing and suspect. For each, the flash and gleam provided a window to lost ideas of Modernity, highlighting instead their own period's wavering confidence in 'the future'. The Art Deco revival's apparently frothy exercise in nostalgia introduced cultural subversion with a winking nudge.

Warhol had jettisoned his Tiffany lamps in favour of Art Deco by the early 1960s. While his Factory on East Forty-Seventh Street in New York is normally associated with its space-age silver foil decor, it was also a shrine to the artist's earliest Deco finds. A curvaceous 1930s couch dominated the main room, serving as a veritable magnet for Warhol and his protégés. Other Deco artefacts lurked around the Factory's edges, including an elaborate 7-foot-high neo-classical Art Moderne bookcase; by the time that *New*

Claes Oldenburg, *Profile Airflow*, 1969.

York magazine profiled Warhol's collecting in 1973, his Factory was referred to as a 'famous storehouse of Deco loot'. Warhol himself, however, rarely acknowledged his obsession publicly. He lent to museum exhibitions liberally and anonymously, and he routinely suggested that his assistant Billy Linich had simply found his 'junk', from 1939–40 World's Fair pretzel holders to Puiforcat Silver, on the street. Warhol actually sought out Deco works with the same tenacity as the collectors who had helped to bring back Art Nouveau to prominence in the previous decade; although he publicly played down his acquisitions, for him, as for the earlier Nouveau collectors, such activities were also self-defining. As he half-seriously told the writer David Bourdon, 'I can't put it in terms of money . . . It's my life'.[18]

However surreptitious, Warhol's collecting drew popular attention to the revival. Sophisticated collectors blamed the artist's films for spreading 'the contagion for the thirties – of which the itch for Art Deco is a clear compulsion – far and wide'.[19] Warhol's own Art Deco pieces indeed appeared frequently in his films; the gritty *Couch* (1964), for instance, starred his red-upholstered, graciously curving 'super-thirties movie-star couch'.[20] Later films like *L'Amour* (1973), made in conjunction with Paul Morrissey, were shot in the Deco-filled Paris apartment of Karl Lagerfeld. When asked in 1971 if he would sell any of his collection, Warhol responded with a resounding no, emphasizing that 'we're using it for all our own movies . . . we're still in the nineteen thirties. We started with silents. Soon we will get up to the nineteen forties'.[21] Even the Empire State Building attracted Warhol's restless camera. *Empire* (1964) used over-exposed film to record the Art Deco structure over the course of a night, beginning shortly after sundown and ending some seven hours later. Warhol's movie represented for the building a kind of cinematic comeback; its striking architecture had been absent from the movies since *King Kong* (1933).

Long entranced with 1930s cinema, Warhol spent his childhood collecting movie magazines and signed publicity photos of his favourite stars. Screen icons such as James Cagney and Ginger Rogers graced his early silkscreens, and he admitted that he discovered Art Deco 'through all those thirties movies on TV, I guess'.[22] While granting that the famous silver foil decoration of his first Factory might evoke futuristic science fiction and the space age, he also insisted that 'silver was also the past – the Silver Screen – Hollywood actresses photographed in silver sets'.[23]

Though fixated with these films, Warhol's own films were nothing like the slick commercialism that characterized Depression-era cinema; the rough cuts and grainy photography of Factory films were the antithesis of Hollywood's inter-war polish. East Village transvestites portrayed Hollywood vamps in *Lupe* (1964), based loosely on the life of the 1920s and '30s Mexican star Lupe Velez. The trio of *Harlot* (1965), *More Milk Yvette* (1965) and *Hedy* (1966) featured the drag queen and performance artist Mario Montez playing the 1930s stars Jean Harlow, Lana Turner and Hedy Lamar respectively. The explicit, even voyeuristic, handling of sex, meanwhile, utterly refuted the chaste and guileless Hays-era romances. Like Robert Cottingham's tungsten-lit marquees or the faded tawdriness of Self's Deco-era cinema interiors, Warhol's films recalled archaic forms of Art Deco's flash and gleam glamour but also the gritty inventiveness of the 1960s.

While Warhol imperfectly evoked 1930s cinema, Lichtenstein recalled the Art Deco years as a 'sort of cartoon era'.[24] Like Warhol, Lichtenstein was fascinated with Depression-era cinema; the rhythmic exactitude in the helmeted soldiers of *Preparedness* recalls images from his own collection of stills from Busby Berkeley musicals. But for Lichtenstein, Art Deco also presented a 'Buck Rogers' way of approaching art and architecture.[25] As Dalí's *Arts* article suggested, Art Deco evoked conflicting ideas of Modernity that fascinated him.

From 1965 to 1970 Lichtenstein repeatedly dealt with Deco style and themes in his 'Modern' style. Upon completing *This Must Be the Place* (1965), his tribute to the 1930s futurism of the World's Fair, he 'started looking at actual objects of the thirties – architecture, jewelry, furniture – and found a lot of material, that's how I got into it'.[26] From the expressive zigzags of paintings like *Modern Painting with Clef* (1967), to the polished brass forms of *Long Modern Sculpture* (1969), Art Deco dominated his Modern style, culminating with large 'narrative' murals like *Preparedness* and *Peace Through Chemistry* (1970). Lichtenstein occasionally cited Fernand Léger and the Bauhaus as sources, but most of his knowledge of the inter-war years came from fragments of popular culture. When he began his Deco-inspired work in 1965, the period remained unnamed; he referred to it simply as 'the thirties'. Like Warhol, he amassed a significant collection of 1930s 'junk', including furnishings, jewellery and publicity photos, while also delving into period guides to architectural ornament, like the Libby-Owens-Ford Glass Company's *Fifty-Two Ways To Modernize Main Street With Glass* (1935).

Preparedness emphasizes Lichtenstein's ambivalent nostalgia for the period's fresh, confident faith in machine-age progress. Its massive wheel spokes recall Art Deco's stylized sunbursts, the tilting girders double as energetic zigzags, while the gleam on an aeroplane window becomes a series of dynamic diagonal striations. Yet Lichtenstein's process relates more to Titian than the machine shop; unlike Warhol's embrace of automated production processes, Lichtenstein remained rooted in the craft tradition. Instead, he responded viscerally to the period's faded glamour, as well as its ethos that 'man could work with the machine to obtain a better living and a great future'.[27] Suggesting that Deco's angular and abstracted forms now seemed 'naïve', Lichtenstein saw 'something humorous in being that logical and rational about a work of art'.[28] Five hundred years earlier, Lichtenstein's triptych format would have suggested a religious altarpiece, with images of Christ's sacrifice and mankind's redemption replacing its mechanized smokestacks. Supplanting a tale of Christian redemption with comic-strip warriors, he gently exposes the faith of machine-age optimism, while wistfully recalling their confidence.

'They thought they were modern', he said in 1967. 'We don't think that we are modern in the same way now.'[29]

History as a Hall of Mirrors

Intoxicated by Deco's machine-age associations, Lichtenstein also asserted the 1930s style's relation to Minimal sculpture. 'I'm kind of humorously making a relationship between the two', he said.[30] Minimalist art of the 1960s embodied an analytic intellectualism seemingly at odds with the transitory whimsy of the Deco revival. But to observant critics, Lichtenstein's analogy was no joke; Sidney Tillim hailed Frank Stella's new shaped and saturated canvases as a more cerebral approach toward 'a thirties feeling for design'[31] than Lichtenstein's own 'Modern' works. Describing Stella's 'Protractor' series of 1968, including *Basra Gate II* (*c.* 1968), the art historian Robert Rosenblum, too, cited their 'appropriate architectural ambience', linking the works with 'that great decorative ensemble of the "modernistic" 1930s, Radio City Music Hall'.[32] The anthropomorphic geometry of Carl André, Donald Judd and Robert Morris, along with Stella, introduced a Minimalist vocabulary that indeed echoed the streamlined geometry of the Deco style. For Pop artists like Lichtenstein and Warhol, Art Deco provided subversive parody, but the Minimalists, most notably Robert Smithson, suggested that Art Deco challenged Modernity's very role in history.

A second-generation Minimalist, Smithson exploded conceptions of time and history through the prismatic mirror of popular Modernism. Although Smithson owned Bevis Hillier's *Art Deco* (1968), his knowledge largely derived from his immediate built environment. Rambling around New York and his home town of Passaic, New Jersey, Smithson exhaustively photographed Deco relics. Images of the extravagantly fluted sconces and steeped ceilings of the Twentieth Century Fox Building in Manhattan, which Smithson haunted for its Deco-era art-house cinema, and the geometric rails and finials of the Chrysler Building's staircases formed a small part of the photographic files that documented the Deco backdrop to his daily activities. These assemblages of snapshots of 1920s and 1930s buildings, many taken during the outings that he called 'field trips', led to his understanding the structures as concrete expressions of time. In Art Deco, Smithson found striking visual and material analogies that supported his interest in the cyclical nature of time as expressed through mirrors, refracted imagery and crystalline structures.

'Ultramoderne', Smithson's paean to Art Deco architecture in the September–October 1967 issue of *Arts* magazine, lauded 'bewildering and . . . remote New York Deco apartment buildings, including The Century, The Majestic, The Eldorado', as well as Radio City Music Hall.[33] The title itself combined the French period term *moderne* with an obscure footnote in the biography of Jorge Luis Borges, who was briefly part of the 1920s 'ultraist' literary group. Smithson shared the Minimalists' attraction to cogent geometric forms; in 'Ultramoderne' he noted that the 'paradigmatic' authority of Art Deco buildings rested on 'repetition and serial order'.[34] His accompanying photographs of the Century Apartments, for instance, focused on the building's 'countless variations of brickwork', highlighting the jutting corners and stepped patterns of its ridged window casings. At the Chrysler Building, too, he focused on a simple repeated zigzag line, recalling the stylized lightning bolts of the lobby's staircase handrail, which itself suggests his current sculptural works.

Indeed, the stepped blocks of Smithson's *Alogon* series (1966) not only imply meticulous repetitive geometry but also the stepped pyramid, or ziggurat. While several of his contemporaries, for instance Joe Tilson and Sol LeWitt, worked with or wrote about ziggurat shapes,[35] Smithson established a singular connection to the subject. From the shape of the artist's *Ziggurat Mirror* (1966) to the stepped architectural embellishments that ornament his *Museum of the Void* drawing (1969), he explored the form and its implications obsessively. When the editors at *Arts* magazine allowed

Smithson to design the 'Ultramoderne' page spreads, he composed the text into a ziggurat shape, emphasizing the motif by illustrating the article with frames from Warhol's *Empire*. The ziggurat shapes that Smithson perceived in Manhattan buildings resonated with associations from Aztec temples and Mesopotamian towers to Paul Frankl's skyscraper furniture and John Storr's sculpture. In 'Ultramoderne', Smithson praised such forms as the 'square spiral' shapes from the 1930s.[36]

Art Deco provided Smithson with a philosophical lattice encompassing both time and history,[37] and hinted at how changing approaches acknowledging the past would in turn shape ideas of retro. For Smithson, Art Deco's slick, reflective surfaces equated with his use of crystals as a metaphor for understanding time as an organic and generative structure; 'the thirties', he argued, were 'a decade fabricated out of crystal and prisms'. Likening Deco architecture's glossy aesthetic with the 'tarnished reflections' of a 'Hall of Mirrors', Smithson argued that the style evoked 'an obsolete future' that was simultaneously backward and forward looking. 'There are two types of time', he wrote, 'organic (Modernist) and crystalline (Ultraist)'; Smithson called the latter sensibility 'trans-historical'.[38]

Smithson admired the interest of 1930s architects in design practices outside the Western tradition. Referring to what he called the period's 'archaic ontology', Smithson believed that the Ultramoderne was 'in contact with the many types of monumental art from every major period – Egyptian, Mayan, Inca, Aztec, Druid, Indian, etc.'[39] He also saw the period's eclectic quotation of multiple styles, often in a single building, as implicitly questioning Modernist doctrine.[40] As he concluded in 'Ultramoderne', 'nothing is new, neither is anything old'.[41] More than Lichtenstein, Warhol and the Pop artists, Smithson's embrace of Art Deco pointed not only towards a new method of measuring and envisioning historical periods but indeed suggested a new approach to understanding history itself.

The Deco Echo in Popular Culture

On May Day 1971 a bomb exploded in the London boutique Biba. The Angry Brigade, a loosely organized group that had carried off similar small bomb attacks on police stations and government offices, quickly took responsibility with a press release to *The Times*. While their missive espoused an uncertain mix of Marxism and anarchy, it also condemned Biba's retro style, contending that 'all the sales girls in the flash boutiques are made to dress the same and have the same makeup, representing the 1940s. In fashion as in everything else capitalism can only go backwards – they've nowhere to go – they're dead.'[42] That the retro invention of Art Deco could help motivate a violent group whose stated targets included 'fascism and oppression' indicates not only retro's ubiquity in popular culture but also its powerful presence by the early 1970s, successful less as a historical movement but particularly potent as both a cultural and marketing phenomenon.

Anything but dead, in the late 1960s retro's consumer magic transformed once disdained Art Deco collectibles into prized 'avant-garde antiques'; the Sonnabend Gallery in New York, whose stable included Arman and Gilbert and George, saw fit to offer 1930s enamel cigarette cases and vases.[43] From *Bonnie and Clyde* (1967), Warren Beatty's tale of Depression-era bank robbers, to the fashion model Twiggy's iconic beret, Deco and retro were assuming both economic and cultural significance. True to retro's selective memory, the older period was reinvested with a new swagger and bristled with ahistorical panache. Biba's 'George Raft trousers' and the gangster pinstripe suits donned by both men and women were avidly worn by the fashion-conscious. While the previous Art Nouveau revival had been shaped by both traditional dealers, collectors, journalists and scholars, Art Deco represented the unusual phenomenon of a historical vision shaped largely by non-historians.

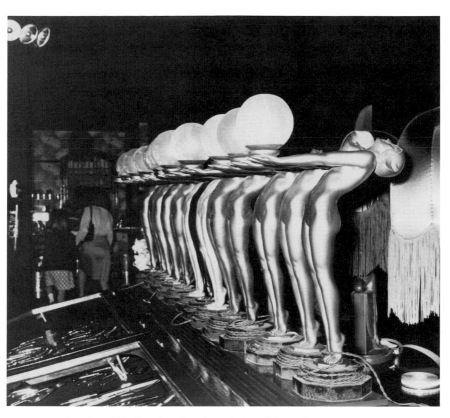

Interior of the London department store Biba, early 1970s.

Just as 1930s cinema initially influenced both the art and the collecting habits of Lichtenstein and Warhol, 1960s stage and film directors combed the older period for inspiration. By the late 1960s and early 1970s the period was memorialized in numerous theatre productions, such as *No, No Nanette*, a giddy revival of a musical of 1925, to films that included Ken Russell's 1930s-style musical extravaganza *The Boy Friend* (1971), starring Twiggy, and Bob Fosse's darker *Cabaret* (1972). But Arthur Penn's *Bonnie and Clyde* had the most pervasive influence, its visual embrace of menacing sub-machine guns and the low-slung Ford V-8 from the early 1930s serving

Faye Dunaway and Michael J. Pollard in *Bonnie and Clyde*, directed by Arthur
Penn, 1967.

as a fashionable backdrop for its anti-establishment heroes. Its popular
influence was so pervasive as to confuse some critics, who suggested that
earlier retro imagery like Lichtenstein's 'Modern' series was actually influenced by the film. Writing in 1968, the critic Sidney Tillim dismissed
Lichtenstein's work as 'Flo Ziegfeld Cubism', and 'painting and sculpture's

The 1930s-inspired 'Gangster look', 1967.

answer to *Bonnie and Clyde*.[44] Arguing that 'millions of Americans, increasingly disturbed by the frenzy of the space age, are now looking back at the nation's past with fascination and longing', *US News and World Report* surmised that American culture *circa* 1973 was taking a 'great leap backward'.[45] But, marking the revival's fashionable advent, it turned the earlier machine-age critique into 'machine-shop chic'.[46]

As the Deco revival inhabited film and fashion, it lost much of the original Pop content that had questioned ideas of Modernity and progress. Nevertheless, audiences in the late 1960s and early 1970s still thrilled to early forerunners of their own mass-media culture. *Bonnie and Clyde* struck many nostalgic notes from 1930s popular culture, from excerpts of Eddie Cantor's popular Depression-era radio show to songs

Ken Russell, *The Boy Friend*, 1971.

sung by the crooner Rudy Vallee. While the film's success spawned a popular soundtrack as well as pop ditties like Georgie Fame's 'Ballad of Bonnie and Clyde' (1967), the period sustained a larger audio revival. At its height in 1971, more than 300 American radio stations were re-broadcasting 1920s and '30s serials, among them 'Fibber and Molly' and 'The Shadow'. Columbia, Decca and other record companies re-released their backlists of big band and jazz recordings. Newer acts, like the ukulele-playing Tiny Tim or the folk-and-blues-inflected Jim Kweskin Jug Band, attracted popular attention, while numerous rock bands, among them Lovin' Spoonful and The Kinks, incorporated old-style jazz and blues arrangements. As Gerald Clarke remarked in 1971, 'sometimes it seems as if half the country would like to be dancing cheek to cheek with Fred Astaire and Ginger Rogers in a great ballroom of the '30s. The other half yearns to join Humphrey Bogart and Ingrid Bergman on a back-lot Casablanca of the '40s.'[47]

Advertisers, publishers and marketing pundits took note; Art Deco graphic design was the perfect pitchman for a sophisticated audience. Though not delving into a complicated critique of Modernity, latter-day admirers saw the style's 'hard-edged sheen and colorless glitter' as representing a new kind of nostalgia that was 'uncompromising and unsentimental'.[48] Hard-edged and metallic, by the 1960s Art Deco suggested a style that was self-consciously modern but also quaintly archaic.

As Jean W. Progner of *Print* magazine reported in the article 'Art Deco: Anatomy of a Revival' (1971), 'designers and their clients in every area from advertising to architecture have bought the box labeled "Art Deco"'.[49] For most designers this box contained an evocative group of stylish motifs and typefaces. By the early 1970s fashion-conscious publications like *Gentlemen's Quarterly, Evergreen, Rags, Changes* and *Vista* introduced hard-edged geometric borders, stylized fountain and rainbow motifs, and slick Futura-inspired typefaces to construct graphic identities that evoked the

Who knows everybody on King's Road?
Mademoiselle Dubonnet, that's who!

Mademoiselle Dubonnet, dolly bird in london town, is at ease in trendy restaurants, posh private clubs, and his lordship's manor house. Try to keep up with her!

An advertisment for Dubonnet, *c.* 1967.

1920s and '30s. Milton Glaser's hugely popular Bob Dylan poster, gleefully mixing colourful Islamic patterning with a black silhouette inspired by Marcel Duchamp, also introduced the typeface Babyteeth. Modelled on

Twiggy in a 1930s
revival dress and
beret, c. 1967.

lettering that the designer saw while visiting Mexico City, the jazzy, angular sans-serif face was quickly associated with the Deco era. But, as 1960s
advertisers for Dubonnet scrambled to achieve a Deco-inspired identity,
they communicated a kind of non-sentimental nostalgia adamant in its
modernity but also hopelessly dated. While subtly ridiculous it still carried
a self-confident glamour that, as Anne Hollander remarked in 1974, was
'somehow wonderfully appealing to the taste of the present moment'.[50]

Fashionable youth clamoured for the style. Claiming that 'the cult of
the past may have developed as an antidote to the cult of the future', Clarke
of *Time* remarked in 1971 that 'after the first moon landings, it might have
been expected that the lords of fashion would try to dress us in shiny vinyl
astronaut suits. Instead, today's with-it woman often looks as if she is
dashing off to the USO or to wrap bundles for Britain.'[51] Art Deco went
mainstream when the model Twiggy, the youthful icon of the age, gushed in
a memoir of 1968 about her 'super new Thirties look', even introducing
adaptations in her own mass-market clothing line.[52] Noting the 'spectacle of

fashions, all apparently lifted whole out of the Art Deco style', Hollander was struck by how they were 'presented as new. And, of course, they *are* [italics hers] new. They are utterly fresh to anyone under 35'.[53]

While such styles seemed inventive and even original to the young, many old enough to have lived through the original period were dismayed by the ahistorical nature of the Deco revival. As John Canaday in observed in the *New York Times*,

> the Depression years and the American bacchanal that led to them are distressing memories except to young people who know them through the second-hand memory of books, movies, and the decorative arts. The young can regard the horrors of the jazz age and the terrors of the breadline with the same interest and equanimity that anyone can feel about the bloodletting of the French Revolution.[54]

Aware that 'the eye of memory takes in 1936 and the elegance of an Astaire dance or the froth of a Lubitsch comedy; it is blind to the Depression breadlines', Clarke remarked that 'at a certain distance, vision fades and imagination takes over'.[55]

Like flagpole sitting or goldfish eating in the 1920s, many 1960s revivalists blindly adopted Art Deco motifs as a fad, little understanding their historical associations. The designers, art directors and journalists most closely associated with the Deco 'revival' acquired little knowledge of the earlier period's eclectic visual sensibility beyond their particular fascinations. Hillier, who introduced the term to a general audience in his monograph *Art Deco*, avoided giving a full-scale definition of the style. When the graphic designer Edward Benguiat began modelling typefaces on the lettering that embellished New York's Radio City Music Hall and the RCA Building's Rainbow Room, he was astonished to find himself declared an 'Art Deco expert' by historians and critics. Indeed, Hillier himself travelled from London to New York to learn more about the style from Benguiat.

Though pleased by the new attention, many of the artists who had worked in the unnamed style during the 1920s and '30s were confounded by the term 'Art Deco'. The Paris exhibition of 1966 that used this name limited itself to works from the Paris exhibition of 1925, but Art Deco quickly came to mean much more. Lynn Ward, an American illustrator active in the 1930s, made no attempt to hide his bewilderment when asked to describe the style by *Print* magazine in 1971. Claiming ignorance, he modestly assumed 'that this was a generally accepted designation of an era of art history of which my lack of qualifications as a student had kept me in ignorance'. Alfred Tulk, an American painter who worked commercially during the inter-war years, was equally perplexed, but more philosophical, when he spoke with Print. Tulk also declared no knowledge of the Art Deco period but surmised 'that "periods" are mostly named in retrospect'.[56]

As the revival gained momentum, it also gathered critics. When *Time* magazine asked the novelist Gore Vidal to comment on the new nostalgia in 1971, he insisted that 'it's all made up by the media. It's this year's thing to write about.'[57] For many cultural commentators, the Art Deco revival was synonymous with 'fad' and 'fashion'. Moreover, designers employing its style were accused of 'unoriginality', and even aesthetic 'whoring'.[58] As the graphic artist Norman Green argued,

> there are too many designers working in the Art Deco style just because it's popular, even though they've no personal feeling for it. Because they've nothing of their own to add to it, they're soon bored by it and start looking for some new fad. These are the people who are always pushing for change without invention.[59]

Nostalgia is a shallow sentiment, and both artists and social commentators began to criticize such revivalism, suggesting that history and historical styles were being recycled and applied to new contexts indiscriminately. The typographer Ernest Hoch denounced the latest revival trend as 'crude fashion-mongering'; in his view designers and artists too often relied on 'a superficial adoption of old formalisms'.[60] Indeed, the last incarnation of the Biba boutique was dominated by Deco but leavened with Art Nouveau bentwood furniture, as well as pillows and baskets evocative of a Middle Eastern kasbah. In Progner's article Milton Glaser defended historical eclecticism, asserting that 'there simply is no belief nowadays in "correct," "true" or even "suitable" styles or aesthetic philosophies'.[61] Instead, he argued, historical styles were merely labels that carried 'very little meaning'.[62] Certainly stylistic mixing afforded the opportunity to inflect familiar forms from the past with paraphrase and parody, even as it decontextualized and even disregarded what some felt to be a style's core being.

With increasingly serious and sustained attention paid to Art Deco, designers, journalists and dealers created a historical style that would subsequently become the subject of traditional academic study. In 1971 Alloway suggested that 'taste for the period has outdistanced the study of it'.[63] By the next year, however, Natalie Gittelson wrote in *Harper's Bazaar* that

> Art Deco has moved into a whole new, non-Campy phase of life. Critical interest is up. Prestige is up . . . perhaps the Campy craving for flashy was there when it all began – Art Deco's Phase I. But that's no longer where it's at today. Today, Art Deco has become serious, historical and, in two words, no joke.[64]

But others worried that the era's loaded economic and political associations had been completely overlooked and its enduring legacy in popular culture badly misunderstood. Few in the mainstream shared the Angry Brigade's animus towards Biba's pre-war revivalism. But, as Robert Pincus-Witten noted in an article in *Artforum* in 1970, Deco's chauvinism and racism went largely unchallenged in its popular revival. While much that passed as the retro revival of Art Deco was formed 'on the basis of pure visceral response', he wrote, the style yet required 'hard scholarly attention. We are, in fact, at that moment in taste when the former imposes the latter as a moral responsibility.'[65]

CHAPTER THREE

Fabricated Fifties

On the fourth day of the Woodstock Festival of 1969, just before Jimi Hendrix's celebrated finale, the stage was held by a group of unknown undergraduates from Columbia University. But these students were not from the SDS (Students for a Democratic Society), leaders of a revolt that had rocked the campus the previous year. Instead, the rock-'n'-roll revivalist group Sha Na Na bombarded the audience with tightly choreographed versions of 1950s classics like 'Teen Angel' and 'At the Hop'. The festival's unlikely scene stealers sported dated looks, including greased ducktails, white socks and cigarettes rolled into T-shirt sleeves. Sha Na Na's impossibly upbeat and exuberant version of the 1950s seemed the opposite of the arty psychedelia and hard rock that characterized Woodstock. Their popularity would only increase; less than a decade later the group hosted an enormously popular weekly television show. Just as the group play rock-'n'-roll standards with amphetamine hype, retro revivalism was recycling the past at an impossibly fast rate.

The mechanism for retro revivals was already in place – the only question was which aspect of the modern past would be resurrected next. Even

The American rock revivalists Sha Na Na, *c.* 1975.

so, the revival of 1950s culture was greeted with a measure of disbelief. Disconcerted by its advent, *Time* magazine observed that 'first the '20s, '30s, and '40s, gleaming with just enough romantic distance, were conjured in theater, art and fashion. Now the nostalgia nuts seem to be closing the gap with the present. That dreary decade, the '50s, is apparently being dusted off for a revival.'[1] Lacklustre to some, raucously rebellious to others, the era revived in the early 1970s was hardly cohesive. Beginning in the late 1940s and ending in the early 1960s, it was not even a decade. But, like earlier retro revivals, such technicalities scarcely bothered the pop historians who fuelled the resurrection of the era.

Managing to charm and aggravate in equal measure, retro was expanding its appeal, but it was also marching to the beat of marketers and an entertainment industry eager to reinvent the modern past. With its roots in Teddy Boy survivals and a resurgent interest in the origins of rock-'n'-roll, this populist retro resurrection continued the marketable Campiness of the Art Nouveau and Art Deco revivals of the 1960s. The Broadway musical *Grease* (1972) and the television series *Happy Days* (1974), as well as countless high-school and university 'sock hops', dance and rock 'n' roll revival tours, blended gloss with dross. At the time, the 1950s revival was thought to mark a shift away from counter-cultural idealism. As Jack Kroll of *Time* magazine observed in 1972, 'the old music, with its Buddy Holly hiccups, its Little Richard yodels, its yackety-yacks and Sha Na Nas, has been reissued, repackaged and reenlisted in the drive of a titanically self-conscious generation to get a firm grip on its identity'.[2] But the revival also represented a clash between communal and personal memory; as the commentator Frank Heath remarked in 1971, 'fifteen years only begins the aging process for fine nostalgia'.[3] Nevertheless, as retro began to revive periods that were well within living memory, it also perceived flaws in the recent past. Immersing oneself in the past proved a way to challenge it.

Teddy Boys and Twiggy

In 1968 the ageing American rock-'n'-roll star Bill Haley toured Britain, wary that his almost fifteen-year-old hits might not find an audience in 'Swinging London'. When he performed at the Royal Albert Hall in May, he explained to the assembled crowd: 'ever since we arrived here people have

Bill Haley and the Jets appearing before a Teddy Boy audience in the Royal Albert Hall, London, 1968.

asked us one question: "Is Rock and Roll going to come back?" I've replied every time "wait until the Albert Hall on Wednesday. If there is anybody there, it's come back".' In an atmosphere that the British music industry journal *Melody Maker* would later describe as 'supercharged', the brimming crowd affirmed Haley with more than words. Dancing on the stage, sitting on each other's shoulders and waving studded belts, the throng grew almost violent in its enthusiasm; by the end of his performance, Haley ran off the stage, pursued by a swarm of adoring fans. Frightened, he refused to reappear for an encore. His performance at the Royal Albert Hall did more than put his classic single 'Rock Around the Clock' back on the British Top Twenty chart. It also drew attention to Britain's enduring Teddy Boy subculture. The audience, dressed in long 'drape' or leather jackets and narrow trousers and sporting greased hair, seemed like relics from another era. But, as *Melody Maker* mused, the crowd was 'on the brink of rioting to music, unchanged for over ten years, played by men who were old enough to be somebody's dad. Rock and Roll Revival be damned – judging by last Wednesday's turn-out it never died!'[4]

For members of Britain's vibrant and anti-establishment Teddy Boy subculture, Haley's concert was like a visitation; such high-voltage events also gave retro a rebellious swagger, spurring a '50s revival in the early 1970s. A generation earlier, the Teddy Boys had turned a post-war fashion trend into a significant cultural statement. Shortly after World War Two, Savile Row, the London street where the high-class tailors were situated, initiated the revival of Edwardian jackets trimmed with half collars of velvet. Itself a curious intimation of retro revival, the style had developed in homosexual circles and was briefly associated with officers in His Majesty's Guards, but it was never accepted by the middle classes. It was, however, worn brashly by young men in the working-class suburbs. Called Teds or Teddy Boys after Edward VII's pet name, by the early 1950s these men wore the clothing style as a statement of rebellion, much as the zoot suit had been adopted in America some ten years earlier. Often linked with gangs and connected with violence, Teds personified bad-boy glamour. They embraced American rock-'n'-roll for its musical rebellion and quickly became known for their cocky style, affecting imports like the Brylcreemed 'quiffs', as well as lapels lined with hidden pockets for razors.

For Teds of the late 1960s and early 1970s, this '50s style expressed deeply held class affiliations but also became a form of cultural reaction. The Teds were left behind as 1960s British popular culture veered towards the Pop Art of Peter Blake and the elfin presence of Twiggy; the Campy embrace of the recent past that swamped the period contrasted with the earnest fashion cues affected by Teds. As the 1960s progressed, the Teddy Boys persisted even as their ranks thinned. When the *Sunday Times* visited a Ted stronghold, the Black Raven pub in Bishopsgate, in 1970, it observed that 'on Friday and Sunday nights, it's as if the 1960s had never been'.[5] Still

Teddy Boys dancing at a rock 'n' roll revival concert at Wembley, 1972.

gathering at pubs and concerts, Teds loyally maintained their '50s uniform of brightly coloured drape jackets, thick-soled 'brothel creeper' shoes and pots of Brylcreem. Their rituals included observing periods of silence in memory of dead rock-'n'-roll stars. And they clearly felt that they hadn't disappeared. Bob Acland, proprietor of the Black Raven, pointedly told *The Times* that 'the Teds aren't a broken army, all gone down a hole like rats. Why, even Princess Anne went to a rock concert with Nixon's daughter. You can't revive what's never been dead.'[6] Indeed, ageing Teddy Boys were also increasingly imitated by a younger generation attracted by their working-class roots; in the face of increasing immigration, many also saw them as preserving a native British style.

Teddy Boy culture in the late 1960s and early 1970s not only reasserted itself but also proved lucrative. In 1972 a huge rock-'n'-roll festival was held at Wembley Stadium; more than 50,000 fans, both original Teds and their youthful followers, came to hear Chuck Berry, Billy Fury, Bill Haley and Jerry Lee Lewis. Revivalist bands such as The Wild Angels, formed in 1967, also began to draw crowds. Stores like Ted Carroll's Rock On record shop in Camden Town, which opened in 1971, catered to the resurgence of Teddy Boy subculture. When Malcolm McLaren and Vivienne Westwood founded Let It Rock in King's Road in Chelsea in the same year, the boutique became so well known for its narrow drainpipe trousers, pointed winkle-picker boots and Buddy Holly records that the film director Claude Waltham asked Westwood to design the costumes for *That'll Be The Day* (1973), a gritty re-creation of the British 1950s rock scene starring David Essex and Ringo Starr. Graced with a jukebox brimming with 1950s rock classics, it was decorated with an odd blend of 1950s artefacts, including suburban furniture, James Dean memorabilia, film stills from 1950s classics and stacks of old movie and pin-up magazines, such as *Photoplay* and *Spick.*

But the boutique reeked of an oddly transfigured nostalgia. The Chelsea sophisticates who shopped at Let It Rock embraced the period in a manner different from the 35-year-old Teds who frequented the shop. For its more urbane customers, the Teds' style hardly represented a venerable way of life. Instead, it offered an intriguing sartorial gesture, expressing disdain for the status quo. Like Susan Sontag's evocation of the Art Nouveau, there was a power in its subversive scorn of the mainstream. Westwood and McLaren were disappointed by the Teds' fundamentally conservative nature. The Teds avoided political and social radicalism, shunned experimentation and were adamant in their quest for authentic re-creations of their own '50s past. Although Let It Rock's promotional brochure proclaimed that 'Teddy Boys are forever', Westwood began to embroider on the Teds' repertoire. In 1973 the boutique changed its name to Too Fast To Live, Too Young to Die, extending its 1950s stock to include defiantly quirky leatherwear inspired by older film stars like Marlon Brando. Instead of merely surviving into a new era, Ted style was blended with trendy entrepreneurship.

But the Teddy Boy subculture disdained sartorial innovation; for the Teds, the '50s extended into their present lives, both as inspiration and personal memory. Fascinated by their adherence to fixed routines and their veneration of specific objects, which helped to bond the subculture, sociologists began to study the Teds in earnest, noting their festishistic obsession with objects and social alienation.[7] Meanwhile, Ted shoppers at Westwood's King's Road store were increasingly dismayed to find drainpipe trousers sold next to latex gear, and drape jackets held together with safety pins. Such transformations caused friction beyond the occasional disgruntled Ted who scribbled angry graffiti on the storefront. This revival did not encompass a period relegated to the memories of an older generation but rather that of a period barely fifteen years earlier. As survival and revival began to blur and cycles of revival shortened, the revived past began to collapse into the present.

'Innocence' as a Commodity

To some in the mainstream media, the '50s revival may have seemed, as *Newsweek* put it, 'nothing so much as the exhaustion of the hope and energy that fired the '60s'.[8] Black leather jackets, sock hops and *Happy Days* helped to convert a wide audience to the retro revival, translating Ted rebelliousness into Howdy Doody innocence. Noting the hula hoop's resurgent popularity, in 1972 *Life* magazine remarked that the '50s revival was both a seductive celebration and an opportunity for quick-witted entrepreneurs to make money 'hand over hip'.[9] Sceptics initially doubted the persistence of the rock-'n'-roll revival. Called a 'flash in the pan' by critics in the music industry,[10] original performers like Haley were enthusiastically received not only by Teds but also broader audiences. Appearing in black leather, Elvis Presley made a comeback in 1968, his televised Christmas show reminding audiences of his brooding appeal. But other performers had slipped into obscurity; early promoters of the '50s revival spent as much money finding original acts as staging their reappearance.[11] Brimming with gleeful showiness and energetic flair, many older acts began working a 'rock-'n'-roll revival' circuit throughout Britain and the USA during the late 1960s. Radio stations included 'golden oldie' formats and record companies rushed to reissue anthologies of '50s hits. Moreover, new analyses of 1950s rock music anointed the older period; publications like Carl Belz's *The Story of Rock* (1969) and Arnold Shaw's *The Rockin' '50s: The Decade that Transformed the Pop Music Scene* (1974) provided the genre with a new-found critical authority.

A younger generation of fans and performers approached the music half lovingly, half mockingly, as retro. In 1968 Frank Zappa released 'Cruising with Reuben and the Jets', a fond parody of sugary doo-wop. But the best-known group to recall and satirize 1950s tunes remained Sha Na Na, whose synchronized dance moves and vocal harmonies were subtly infused with Camp. George Leonard, the group's leader, described himself as a '22-year-old Susan Sontag buff'.[12] Recalling the group's transformation from Ivy League glee club to television stars, Leonard spoke of a 'vision of a group that would sing only '50s rock and perform dances like the Busby Berkeley films that he 'learned to love in college readings on Camp'.[13] Sensing their tongue-in-check panache, Sha Na Na's first agent urged the group to call themselves 'The Put-Ons'; instead, they opted for a name based on the nonsense lyrics from the song 'Get a Job'. Hailed in *Newsweek* as 'a new breed of entertainer', the group's campy reinterpretation of 1950s rock music appealed to younger audiences even more than '50s stars like Haley or the pianist Fats Domino.[14] When Sha Na Na performed at Woodstock, their precious edginess translated into record contracts, film

The cast of the stage musical *Grease* promote the show at the 1973 London Motor Show, driving a Chrysler Windsor of c. 1950.

appearances and an eventual television show. With success like this, imitators were endemic. Riding the lucrative retro wave, bands like Australia's Daddy Cool, Britain's Showaddywaddy and the American Flash Cadillac and the Continental Kids inspired not only good feelings but were themselves copied; the Junior Cadillacs fashioned themselves after the last. As one of Sha Na Na's founding members recalled, 'we realized that wherever there was this kind of brotherhood, there had to be money'.[15]

Perceiving the same potential, the entertainment industry funded a broader revival in the early 1970s. *Grease*, initially mounted as a summer amateur production in Chicago, was brought to New York and billed as a 'New '50s Rock-'n'-Roll Musical'. Even before *Grease* was adapted to the screen in 1978, other films capitalized on the 1950s revival, including Claude Whatham's *That'll Be the Day* (1973) and *The Lords of Flatbush*

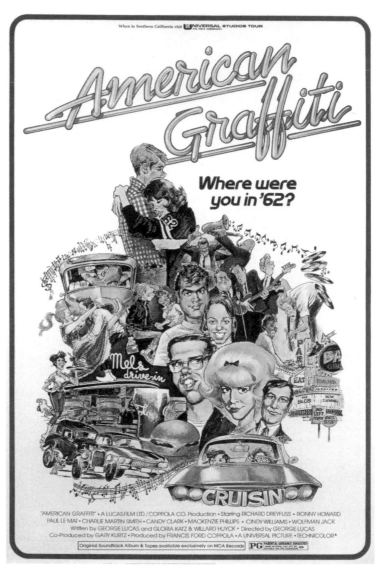

Poster for George Lucas's *American Graffiti*, 1973.

(1974), directed by Martin Davidson and Stephen Verona. But the best-known revivalist film remains George Lucas's *American Graffiti* (1973). Evoking a single night in Modesto, California, in 1962, Lucas's film, set a year before the Beatles arrived in America, extended the range of the 1950s. On its release, the *New York Times* critic Stephen Farber pronounced it to be 'the most important American movie . . . maybe since *Bonnie and Clyde*'.[16] Lucas spent an unprecedented proportion of his film's budget securing the rights to songs already popular on the revivalist circuit, including 'Johnny B. Goode' and 'Rock Around the Clock'. Not only did his deft translation of the rock-'n'-roll revival bolster imitations like the television series *Happy Days*, but it also signalled a growing hunger for a 1950s revival that transcended the energetic flair of its music.

By 1974 *Life*, *Newsweek*, *Saturday Review*, *Time* and the London *Times* all remarked on this revival of the recent past, but also noted that its main audience was quite young. College campuses hosted dress-up 'greaser days', 'Come as you were in the '50s' parties, sock hops and performances by the 1950s children's star Howdy Doody. Students flocked to stores carrying memorabilia from the show. Female co-eds sported strapless cocktail dresses or saddle shoes, while their male counterparts, imitating the retro glamour of Henry Winkler's subversive chic from *Happy Days*, adopted black leather jackets and cut their hair short or greased it back. Centred on clothes, music and film, the youthful revival focused on the earlier period's affluent popular culture.

With their mastery of period details like madras shirts and double Chubby Chuck Burgers, films like *American Graffiti* evoked the period from the point of view of a teenage consumer. Indeed, the 1950s revival emphatically overlooked the period's self-congratulatory pride in its 'culture boom', including surging attendance at the theatre and art museums, as well as the healthy sales of classical records and widely read series like 'Great Books of the Western World', published by the *Encyclopedia Britannica*. Instead, the Teddy Boy subculture fetishized the period's youthful consumer goods,

Howdy Doody's Bob Smith surrounded by memorabilia, *c.* 1970.

A scene from *Happy Days*, *c.* 1980.

including 78-rpm records, crêpe-soled shoes and pots of Brylcreem. Seeing a grand marketing opportunity, advertisers helped to push the Teddy Boys' riotous materialism into American living rooms as 1950s rock replaced the Roaring Twenties as a popular party theme.

Rock 'n' roll revival promoters were among the first to see an opportunity for 'cross-pollination' within the entertainment industry, expanding to sponsor 1950s car shows, sock hops and flea markets that featured unused tubes of hair cream and pristine copies of *Song Hits* magazine. Others quickly followed suit. Radio stations and clothing boutiques sponsored 'class reunion' dances and telephone-booth stuffing contests. One shoe manufacturer, reintroducing a saddle shoe popular in the 1950s, displayed the new footwear on old 78-rpm records and offered a cream-coloured '57 Chevy as a contest prize.[17] Buffalo Bob Smith of *Howdy Doody* touted more than show memorabilia in toy stores; having advertised grape juice in the 1950s, in the early 1970s he peddled cheap wine in a radio commercial. Finding their history a saleable asset, the originator of the Hula Hoop resumed production in 1967; a million were sold in 1972. New businesses were formed, including clothing stores that sold 'vintage' pleated and pegged trousers and companies that custom-built cars based on models of Edsels and Cadillacs. In Britain, it was the vision of American high school proms, hot rods, drive-ins and not menacing Teddy Boys that entrepreneurs recalled when opening eateries like 'The Great American Disaster'. The 1950s saw a 'heady, nearly ten-year-long shopping spree, this unabashedly hedonistic orgy of acquiring – this we look back on with tolerance and affection'.[18]

For those too young to remember the original period, the 1950s revival arrived at a time of increasingly bleak economic prospects, and in the wake of the previous decade's turbulent social changes. Noting that *Grease* originally opened in New York to 'a neighborhood crowd' who were 'mostly in their thirties – war babies who had grown up in the '50s and were anxious to recapture their past', the producers of the show saw their audience change quickly. Following its move to a larger theatre on Broadway, the seats were filled by a younger, 'nostalgia-seeking audience' of teenagers, who, in the words of the actress Kathi Moss, are going 'back to the basics'.[19] *Life* magazine was more philosophical, noting how a younger generation was drawn to this revival and claiming that 'pop psychologists – and many of the kids – see the flight to the '50s as a search for a happier time, before drugs, Vietnam, and assassination'.[20]

But the oily pompadours, insignia on gang jackets and blaring rock music that characterized the early revival also evoked working-class aspirations, street gangs and a form of juvenile delinquency that defied the period's conformism. Casually, even insolently, they also signalled, as Jack Kroll of *Time* noted in a 1972 review of *Grease*, a society 'getting ready to become the counterculture' of the 1960s.[21] As one fifteen-year-old explained to *Life* in 1972, 'those greasers were the first freaks'.[22] But, like the leather jacket, this rebellion entered the 1970s with only a mildly menacing patina; its mollifying cuteness muted any rumblings of rebellion, especially in the face of a more recent culture of student protests, race riots and urban guerrillas. 'A year after student antiwar protesters closed dozens of colleges and universities across the country', Andrew H. Malcolm of the *New York Times* observed in 1971, 'thousands of the same youths are caught up in a new pursuit – nostalgia for the good old days'.[23] In 1973 *Time* praised *American Graffiti* as the leading edge of 'a certain nostalgia' that 'began inching its way into memory like a balm'.[24]

When the Teds' dissonant rebelliousness was drowned out, some of the revival's edginess was obliterated. Teenage hot rods and tawdry neon honky tonks quickly acquired iconic status but also carried more innocent associations. When the lyric 'Rock Around the Clock' originally opened the film *Blackboard Jungle* in 1955, it was an anthem for the film's switchblade-wielding gangs that terrorized an urban high school; as the theme of both *American Graffiti* and *Happy Days* in the mid-1970s, the song became more tonic than threatening. Once indicative of teenage rebellion, by 1972 a staid

Newsweek was calling such rock'n'roll 'innocent' in comparison to the 'raunchy' music of the early 1970s.[25] Chart-topping contemporary songs also gave a wistful nod to such older music from 'American Pie' (1972), Don MacLean's plaintive ode to Buddy Holly, to the Carpenters' 'Yesterday Once More' (1973). In *Time* magazine, one of *Grease*'s original creators recollected the 'innocence of the period', characterizing his youth in 1950s Chicago as a dull but peaceful period 'when the only thing kids knew about the president was that he played golf and had trouble with his intestines, and the biggest tragedy in life was if you didn't get your dad's car for the drive-in'.[26] Themes of lost innocence connected this revival with the earlier resurrections of Art Nouveau and Art Deco. Describing the carefree teenagers in the stage play *Grease*, Kroll detected that 'Rydell High becomes a vivid and funny microcosm of an age already as touching as the era of "No, No, Nanette"'.[27]

For 'those who grew up in the '50s, the happy images of that decade are a positive reassurance – a reclaiming of fading youth'.[28] Many of the artists and collectors participating in the previous Art Deco revival were attracted to the inter-war period of their early childhoods. As the *New York Times* noted in 1970, well-known collectors of Art Deco, for instance, Andy Warhol, Roy Lichtenstein, Barbra Streisand and Donald Judd, 'were born between the wars when the style was young. Who indeed growing up during the Depression years could forget the Aztec temples that framed radios?'[29]

Not only did the deluge of leather jackets, pedal pushers, Marilyn Monroe calendars and Marlon Brando motorcycle posters sweep a tide of retro revival, but they also announced the recycling of the very recent past. Posters for Sha Na Na's appearances on college campuses evoked what one band member called a 'pre-political teenage Eden', announcing 'Jocks! Freaks! ROTC! SDS! Let there be a truce! Bury the hatchet (not in each other)! Remember when we were all little grease balls together.'[30] A Harvard professor told the *New York Times* at the time: 'today's college student missed out on the college life of panty raids, clubs, and big weekends. They had politics instead . . . some students may feel they missed something.'[31]

Reinventing the Day Before Yesterday

From the OPEC oil crisis to Watergate, America in 1973 seemed to be unravelling. When *American Graffiti* appeared in August of that year, its camera lingered lovingly on the glinting chrome of rocket-shaped tailfins and swollen extravagances of gas-guzzling cruisers. Awed audiences noted its evocation of a time untroubled by oil rationing and diminutive fuel-economizing imports. School sock hops and restored hot rods evoked happier days. But for some critics and historians, the past was collapsing into the present.

'Who wants to be bothered remembering the '50s?', insisted Edith Oliver in the *New Yorker*, speaking for a generation of cultural commentators in 1972. 'The '30s and '40s, yes, and the '60s, yes indeed, but the 1950s made one of the dullest decades on record and are better forgotten.'[32] Even a profile in *Newsweek*, 'Back to the '50s', agreed that 'in the grand sweep of American history, the 1950s were one of the blandest decades ever'.[33] For historians, the 1950s was a dreary period accented only by memories of Joe McCarthy and emotional and sexual repression, not Bill Haley, greased hair and leather jackets. As early as 1960, the historian Eric Goldman looked back on what he called the 'stuffy' decade, announcing in *Harper's Magazine*: 'Good-Bye to the '50s – and Good Riddance'.[34] Commenting on the era's freewheeling consumption in *America in the Sixties: An Intellectual History* (1968), Ronald Berman recalled a 'bloated '50s in which a nation became trapped by its own affluence'.[35] As the 1960s unfolded, the rise of the free speech movement and the New Left made the previous decade seem not just antiquated but somewhat menacing. By 1971 the historian

Fred J. Cook's survey of the period's politics was entitled *The Nightmare Decade: The Life and Times of Senator Joe McCarthy*. History's official chroniclers had passed judgement on the decade – and the verdict was resoundingly negative.

If the 1950s were remembered as a visual style, through popular entertainment and fashion, the revival's reduction of the recent past into a simple ten-year block also emphasized the rapid acceleration of history. Historians had sliced epochs of time into decades since the early nineteenth century. By the 1930s books like Frederick Lewis Allen's *Only Yesterday: An Informal History of the 1920s* (1931), which charted the rise in the previous ten years of the foxtrot and bobbed hair, proved that chronological decades could be used to chart the recent past, and especially its popular culture, without having to digest its complex character. Even as it unfolded, the Art Deco revival was often facetiously referred to as 'Thirties style'. This incremental approach to history helped to encourage the rapid repackaging of the modern past. 'We are teetering on the edge of nostalgia shock', fretted Frank Heath in the *Saturday Review* in 1971. Noting the shallowness of decade-based revivalism, he observed that

> the Twenties, a veritable mother lode of memories, are very nearly depleted. The Thirties, never a rich decade, are also overworked. As for the Forties, few people long for a war right now and that puts us well into the Fifties, a scant fifteen years ago . . . we'll soon be nostalgic for 1965, then 1969, and soon we'll be saying, 'You think that was something? You should have been alive ten minutes ago!'[36]

Drawing on popular memory, *American Graffiti* ads asked: 'Where were you in '62?' While few in the film's target audience had reached adulthood in that year, the 1950s revival did give pause to the older generation.

During the Art Deco revival, older observers were dismayed that this resurrection of the past was blind to Depression bread lines and the rise of Nazism. The 1950s retro was equally oblivious to McCarthy hearings and 'duck-and-cover' bomb drills. Bevis Hillier, whose *Art Deco* had helped to spur the revival of inter-war design some fifteen years earlier, noted how Hula Hoops, clutch coats and rock 'n' roll created a myopic 1950s. 'Now at last I begin to understand why my parents' generation is unable to share much of my enthusiasm for Art Deco – the style of the period just before my birth. What to me is "nostalgia" (for a period I never knew) is to them just experience.'[37] Not only was it true, as Gerald Clarke of *Time* insisted, that 'vision fades and imagination takes over',[38] but many of those who lived through the period had difficulty reconciling the revival with their own memories. Shocked at the happy-go-lucky imagery associated with the revival, another writer for *Time*, Stefan Kanfer, insisted in 1974 that 'no one can begrudge the decade its place in the sun; yet anyone over the age of 25 may object to the prefix Fabulous . . . Coming of age in the '50s was something less than storied. It was rather like taking a walk in a fog.'[39] As Richard Lingeman recalled, 'the '50s under Ike represented a sort of national prefrontal lobotomy: tail-finned, we Sunday drove down the superhighways of life'.[40]

Although some in the audience of the stage production of *Grease* were, according to its creator, 'astonished that this is the past already', they greeted it not so much with wistfulness as bemusement.[41] 'The tone of the show is tongue-in-(and-out-of-) cheek,' one reviewer gushed, 'and perhaps it is true that the best way to parody the '50s is simply to imitate them.'[42] A theatrical presence characterized Sha Na Na too; in 1971 one music critic observed 'a genuine rock repertory company whose theatrical program of '50s anthems is high-powered, loving, semi-satire'.[43] However mild, it was this element of parody that provided a distancing mechanism, allowing the recent past to be transformed into collective memory.

Yet retro suggested more than an engagement with the past; the future was also beginning to change. Suggesting that recalling the recent past was something that youth could 'relate to and which they can control', in 1971 a Stanford psychology professor, Philip Zimbardo, told the *New York Times*: 'today's youth is threatened by an uncertain future, alienated from traditional values and turned-off by the hypocrisy and violence they see about them'.[44] As *Horizon Magazine* suggested a year later, 'people begin to remember the 1950s not as they recall them but as they have been re-created for them. This is what makes the newly minted myth of the 1950s so remarkable and so Modern. It's a myth about a time that half the country has lived through, a myth, as it were, about the day before yesterday.'[45]

Mode retro

But, through the early 1970s, the 1950s were not the only corner of recent memory to be resurrected. Almost simultaneously, the *mode rétro* resurrected France's murky war years. A recapitulation of the early 1940s, the *mode rétro* bore a curiously close, if contorted, kinship with the revival of the sock-hopping American 1950s. But the *mode rétro* evolved from memory's inversion, from a collective, willed effort to forget.

The 1940s carried special associations in France; often termed the *années noires*, the German invasion and occupation exposed acrimonious divisions in French society. As the pro-Nazi Right cleaved from the radical Left, the country verged on civil war; the common sense of glorious destiny based on historical continuity and consensus, and France's vision of a national grandeur linking the present to the past, were effectively shattered. Following his joyful reception in Paris in August 1944, Charles de Gaulle conscientiously refashioned the war years into a narrative of vigorous resistance. Tailoring a new myth of France after his own beliefs, de Gaulle asserted that France had liberated herself from the Germans. French memories of the Occupation were suppressed in favour of a Gaullist gloss that emphasized collective struggle and heroism in the face of invasion and tyranny. The myth of *La France résistante* was invented, carefully cultivated and vigorously defended by government and intellectuals alike until the early 1970s.

The ascent of the *mode rétro* coincided with de Gaulle's resignation from the French presidency in 1969. In his wake, a younger generation with few personal memories of the war years researched and reviewed this humiliating period of French history. For some this reinvestigation recapitulated a missing heritage.[46] But many others, mistrustful of accepted beliefs, sought to re-examine France's history in World War Two as a means to indict the older generation.

Based on interviews with survivors and witnesses, this reinvestigation of the war years was prompted by Marcel Ophüls's powerful documentary *Le Chagrin et la pitié* (1969). Employing recorded recollections of the war generation along with photos and newsreels, Ophüls's film probed post-war orthodoxies, suggesting that the French Resistance was much smaller than previously supposed and that contemporaries often held its members in poor esteem. A distinct element of inter-generational strife weaves through the film, yet the sum of its halting interviews and damning newsreels reveals the implausibility of the Gaullist war legend. Ophüls, fired by a state-owned television station after his participation in a crippling strike at the network in 1968, began work on the film in the wake of that year's student and worker riots. Originally conceived for French television, the film was banned from broadcast but eventually played to packed Parisian cinemas during a limited run in 1971.

In newspapers and journals, literature and cinema, music and fashion, Ophüls's work marked the tip of a broader re-evaluation of France's war years that was sweepingly called the *mode rétro*. From films that deprecated the Resistance as cowardly, egotistical and cynical to books that rehabilitated and justified collaborators, the trend filtered through French culture in the post-1968 years. Novels like Patrick Modiano's *La Ronde de nuit* (1968) and *Les Boulevards de ceinture* (1972) plunged readers into a world of

Lacombe Lucien, directed by Louis Malle, 1974.

the French Gestapo and collaborationist journalists. But the *mode rétro* was most keenly felt in the cinema; from 1974 to 1978 approximately 45 French films were set in World War Two, more than the entire previous decade.[47] Movies such as Michel Mitrani's *Les Guichets du Louvre* (1974), which described the mass arrests of the Jewish population of Paris by French police in 1942, and Louis Malle's *Lacombe Lucien* (1974), whose eighteen-year-old protagonist becomes a Nazi collaborator through happenstance, depicted French collaboration vividly. Like *Le Chagrin et la pitié*, they also told their stories through common people, bringing history to life through unremarkable Parisian streets and rural farms.

Termed 'curiously perverse' by critics, this re-examination prompted a vogue in the early 1970s for war-era music and fashion; its romanticization of the war years suggested a form of excoriation and also expiation.[48] Such open discussion of France's Nazi past bred a type of reconfigured nostalgia, echoing the revivals of the Art Nouveau and Art Deco movements, as well as that of the 1950s. Interviewing French youth in 1974, the *New York Times* reported 'a kind of nostalgia among young people who had never lived through the war, who are bored by today and feel they have been somehow cheated of a fascinating and demanding adventure through which their parents lived'.[49]

In the face of their parents' silence about their wartime experiences, France's young listened to their music and tried on their clothes. Hit songs from the war years were rediscovered. Parisian youth scoured flea markets for second-hand German leather coats and ankle-strap shoes. While chic youth like Paloma Picasso resembled Dorothy Lamour in a red turban and her mother's black crêpe dress,[50] *haute couture* designers like Yves Saint Laurent also began to recall Occupied France in collections of the early 1970s. Saint Laurent, who had recently commemorated the protesters manning the 1968 barricades with a women's wear collection that included fringed jackets, trousers and dark, subdued colours, now evoked memories of the 1940s in his *mode rétro* wear. A women's double-breasted 'slack suit', padded shoulders, ankle-strapped platform shoes and 'creole' turban that recalled the 1940s film star Carmen Miranda won the favour of critics with its empowering look.

But much of Saint Laurent's collection included fur wraps, platform shoes and low-cut, tight-fitting dresses that represented a vision of the 1940s dominated by female collaborators rather than Gaullist heroines. Critics admonished his 'tart' or 'World War II floozy look',[51] claiming that he was conjuring 'the streetwalker's 1940s' or 'Forties Camp'. Many in the English-speaking press failed to connect his fashion with historical revisionism; the *New York Times'* fashion correspondent Bernadine Morris asked: 'was Saint Laurent making fun of the 1940s – or the audience? Or was the whole collection one big parody of fashion?'[52] Previously the toast of French couture, Saint Laurent defended himself by calling his critics

A model displays a
double-breasted beige
gabardine trouser suit
by Yves Saint Laurent,
1971.

'narrow-minded and reactionary, petty people paralyzed by taboos'. Saint Laurent draped his clothes in broader cultural rhetoric, arguing against 'people who do not dare to look life in the face and who are assured by tradition'.[53] As if the only way to escape the past's legacy was to confront it, the French *mode rétro* recalled the 1940s, trying to shake off the burden of the past through immersion in it.

Most of Saint Laurent's well-heeled customers did not care to don the wardrobe of war-era prostitutes and climb the ramparts of cultural dissent. But his desire to tap memories of the 1940s cast a shadow beyond the sharp-shouldered silhouette that would be seminal to 1980s fashion. Though not limited to France's youth, the *mode rétro* tapped a nihilist strain within the generation of 1968, recalling the war years with a dark glee that verged on amorality. At least one critic believed that Malle's morally hamstrung Lucien Lacombe was a bell-wether; ignorant of ideology and utterly self-involved, he was hailed as 'a man of today'.[54] Like the homosexuals who had embraced the 'degenerate' Art Nouveau styles a generation earlier, the *mode rétro*'s resurrection of the war era was not only dissonant, but it also suggested a subversive form of power.

When asked in 1971 about his group's remarkable popularity, Sha Na Na's manager replied: 'obviously the past is more simple and less painful than the present. It's been lived through. In a world with very few standards left, the past offers those standards whether you live by them or not.'[55] But the French *mode rétro* presented a past that was ambiguous and complex. French critics like Jean Baudrillard, whose 'History: A Retro Scenario' (1981) suggested that retro helped to form an age of simulation, linked the term to 1970s cinema. While admitting that retro aestheticized fascism's 'filtered cruelty', Baudrillard argued that retro also represented 'the death pangs of the real and of the rational'.[56] The French *mode rétro* ultimately signalled a demythologization, the taking away of meaning. Very much a symptom of its time, the *mode rétro* followed the revolutionary fervour of 1968. When sweeping change failed, it was easy to look back to periods like World War Two when important causes, whether fascist or not, seemed to matter; the period evoked a detached type of nostalgia.

Filtering into Britain in the late 1970s, retro described fashions that embraced both the happy days of the 1950s and the *mode rétro* of occupied Paris. Certainly, Britain and America had flirted briefly with a frothy 1940s revival in the early 1970s. In October 1970 *Esquire* magazine featured a war-era pin-up and the caption 'Welcome back to the '40s: the last time America was happy', and in 1971 Hollywood released *Summer of '42* (1971) and *Carnal Knowledge* (1971), both set in the war years. But, while zoot suits achieved a brief resurgence in popularity, few Vietnam-era youth chose to parody the war's popular culture; unlike the hazy and morally indistinct climate of the French war years, the social certainties of the 1950s were charmed and yet also easily spoofed. It was only when, in the late 1970s, retro revivers took note of the style that expressed 'the high standard of living brought by advancing technology',[57] that the 1950s revival began to resemble the French *mode rétro*, suggesting a darker side to the era, suffused with a broader interrogation of the original period and the values that shaped it.

Fallout from the 1950s

With its curved Plexiglas bubble window and shiny streamlined body, the appearance of a Chantal Meteor 200 jukebox at a Sotheby's auction in London in 1973 drew, in the words of a reporter from the *Sunday Times*, 'the wry smiles and sagging jaws' of onlookers.[58] In 1976 the *Times* proclaimed that 'the '50s are beginning to acquire the sort of attraction that made styles of the Twenties and the Thirties into collectors' pieces'. At Sotheby's the period made its official decorative arts debut not through an Isamu Noguchi table or an Eames sofa, but rather through artefacts of popular culture, such as jukeboxes and nude Marilyn Monroe calendars. 'Jukeboxes do capture the mood of that period so well, I think', mused Philippe Garner, the auction house's expert on twentieth-century decorative art. 'By bringing something like the Chantal into prominence,' he added, 'you hopefully begin to establish that the '50s, like any other, was a definite period in the decorative arts that had a beginning and an end. Its identity begins to crystallize.'[59]

Marked by the reappearance of saddle shoes, sugary doo-wop and tailfins, the 1950s revival was especially promoted by the popular entertainment industry and unfurled rapidly outside the visual arts. Nurtured by the rock-'n'-roll revival and a series of period films, the 1950s revival created a communal myth of the decade. In the popular imagination, the 1950s retro revival translated into 78-rpm records, soda fountains and commodified innocence. But as Garner suggested, the 1950s revival did not immediately coalesce around a distinctive style in art and design. It was only as the period became equated with a distinct visual style that the revival became more subversive.

During the post-war years, the public was dazzled by the growth of applied science, optimistically dubbing theirs 'the jet age' and 'the atomic age'. The ebullient retro revival of bubble-gum, drive-ins and rock 'n' roll in the early 1970s painted the 1950s as an 'unruffled decade that preceded the trauma of the 1960s'.[60] But slang from the 1950s and early 1960s exposed deep-rooted anxieties. While teenagers 'bombed' around in their Chevys, the period's most daring bathing suit was named after an atomic test site, and women's elaborately teased hairstyles were dubbed B52s, after long-range American bombers. As in its jargon, the period's art and design reflected this anxiety more clearly than the early 1950s revival let on.

Watching the revival from a distance, professional art historians and critics emphasized its popularity, but were ambivalent about its implications. Critics like Kim Levin, writing in a special issue of *Arts* magazine in 1974 devoted to the decade, posited: 'the '50s is still dangerous ground – a mine field full of painful yearnings and mixed memories'.[61] In the visual arts, an ebullient, popular but also slightly tainted Modernism wafted through the original period. At mid-century, this style's affiliations with post-war science and technology connected it with a subtext overlooked in the initial revival: the period's nuclear legacy. Instead of the gleaming Chantal jukebox, Levin remembered a special kind of '50s fallout', founded on the 'incomprehensible idea of the Bomb [that] had sunk into people's souls'. For Levin, the only jukebox worth remembering was Allen Ginsberg's reference in the poem 'Howl' (1956) to the Hydrogen Jukebox music.[62]

After fifteen years of war and Depression, the post-war peace, bolstered by economic expansion and the rapid conversion of wartime industry to consumer culture, initiated a period of unprecedented material prosperity. While consumer taste remained fundamentally conservative, the art and design establishment embraced the boldly simple and functional Modernist aesthetic as a commodity that expressed economic affluence and cultural sophistication. Growing out of MoMA's precepts for 'Good Design', the style had earlier provided an easy target for Tiffany revivalists looking for exoticism and personal liberation. Mass-produced yet high-quality, rational designs by well-known Modernists like Eames and Saarinen converted wartime materials, such as moulded plywood and fibreglass, into home furnishings. Although the Good Design movement held limited appeal for the wider public, elements of its style, for instance its simple biomorphic and abstract forms, trickled into popular culture; the cheap, ebullient and notably populist forms of 1950s popular luxury, often called 'populuxe', translated these forms, mixing Modernism with a cheery, if gaudy popular taste. Revelling in colourful plastic 'televisions today from the world of tomorrow' and coffee shops surmounted by soaring, steel-cantilevered roofs that resembled space ports, populuxe combined Modernistic style with new materials and low-cost production methods. Modernism's abstract forms and sleek and simple design vocabulary were accessible to the public, embraced as a widely accessible, optimistic expression of futurism. Vasily Kandinsky's abstractions decorated the Formica countertops in roadside diners; the slick streamlined surfaces that characterized 1920s Bauhaus designs influenced the shape of Whirlpool washing machines in the early 1950s. Broadly, as High Modernism filtered into private and public spaces, and applied science shaped home and work, the future seemed almost within grasp. Anticipating what would come, it was easy to expect that the world would only get better.

This prosperous, easy-going optimism was easily interpreted as 'innocence' by the retro revivalists in the early 1970s. But the older period was shaded by an atomic cloud that tinged much of 1950s literature, art and film, from Ginsberg's 'Howl' to Jackson Pollock's abstractions to *Godzilla* movies. Motifs from atomic physics, like the split atom, appeared on George Nelson Ball Clocks and *Mechanix* comics alike. Recalling the 'taint' that ran through the 1950s, Levin perceived a 'trauma [that] permeated the decade. Behind the good times and happy days loomed the indelible newsreel image of an incredible growing, mushrooming, phallic cloud over the water at Bikini, irrational and horrifying.'[63]

If Levin, writing in *Arts*, insisted that 'except in the field of pop music the revival was premature',[64] most art critics and professional historians shared her repugnance for the period. Rather than reject this taint, though, commercial artists were intrigued by the tense alternation between optimism and gloom that characterized the 1950s. *The Atomic Age* (1975), a visual reference guide for artists written by an American graphic-designer, Marc Arcenaux, chronicled motifs like spiky models of Sputnik. Arcenaux, who earlier had spoofed the period's perceived innocence by designing visual parodies, such as *National Lampoon*'s facetious high-school yearbook in 1964, wittily recalled the designs for Monsanto's plastic house of the future and the Predicta television, as well as abstract parabolas and amoeba shapes. But, remembering the period's biggest irony of all, he also included split-atom motifs, reminding readers that 'as Americans looked to the future with buoyant enthusiasm', they also 'lived under the shadow of a mushroom cloud'. So described, he touched a raw nerve of the original period, but also one that observers in the mid-1970s, as now, have not escaped.[65]

Alternately exciting and frightening, 1950s Modernism and populuxe acknowledged and assimilated a nuclear threat that had not gone away; the retro revival of these visual styles addressed this paradox. Taking their cues from the harlequin diamonds, free-form lettering and unnaturally acidic colours of 1950s record covers, for instance, punk rock promoters looked to adopt, and subvert, 1950s Modernist design. Just as Vivienne Westwood's punk clothing had its roots in Teddy Boy subculture, punk's musical roots lay in the 1950s; punk record companies actively quoted, but also subverted, the earlier period's golden age of sleeve design, recalling the Modernist abstractions of Saul Bass, Alvin Lustig and Alex Steinweiss. The Clash may have splattered their clothes with paint dribbles that recalled Jackson Pollock, but when the cult-cartoonist Ray Lowry designed their *London Calling* cover of 1979, he closely imitated the black-and-white concert photo and pink-and-green block lettering of Elvis Presley's debut album of 1956. While Elvis's iconic cover depicted Presley flailing away in concert, however, Lowry chose an image of Paul Simonon, The Clash's bass player, smashing his guitar against a stage. Punk's subversive reuse of 1950s imagery was even clearer in Lowry's sleeve for the record's single; imitating a pre-1958 HMV record cover, it depicted happy dancers blissfully waltzing, but Lowry's couple skirted under an atomic cloud.

If punk designers were among the first to note subversively the link between 1950s Modernism and applied science, by the late 1970s many artists and designers were increasingly intrigued by the 'technological euphoria of the times'.[66] Italian banal design embraced the Campy reuse of materials like plastic laminates popular in the 1950s, adapting them to bizarre bookcases, tables and couches. The American painter David Salle, whose art pulled images from comics and pulp fiction, television and pornography, parodied the organic pretensions of the period's Modernism in paintings like *Brother Animal* (1983), placing two Eames LCW chairs next to a depiction of a kidney.

Nevertheless, the earlier period's exuberant futurism was most remarked on; as the architecture critic Nayana Currimbhoy rather enviously recalled in 1987, 'in the '50s, technology was the magic carpet, ready to transport human kind into a bright new world'.[67] Epitomized by Googie, the gravity-defying vault-and-cantilevered architecture best exemplified in roadside restaurants, gas stations and motels of the 1950s and early 1960s American West, populuxe's futuristic building style was rediscovered by architects and preservationists in the early 1980s. As architects argued that the buildings' space-age forms were 'as much a symbol of the '50s as Elvis Presley or a '57 Chevy',[68] preservationist groups like the Los Angeles Conservancy, founded in 1984, fought for the first time to protect these buildings from destruction. Evoking from the 1950s a space-age future that seemed almost tangible, Pop-influenced artists such as Kenny Scharf teased the style's futurism in glossy paintings like *Ships* (1979), a depiction of a sign from one Los Angeles coffee shop, complete with a boomerang 'forward look' logo and jagged Googie roofline, silhouetted against a starry night sky.

While such lightly surreal futurism was attractive, it also carried dystopian associations. The American pop group The B-52s, who took their name less from the long-range bombers that Boeing introduced in 1954 than Southern slang for women's bouffant hair styles, gleefully adopted props and clothes from the 1950s and early 1960s. As Karen Schoemer noted in the *New York Times* in 1989, their early albums 'sounded as quaint as an Automat, as hyper-Modern as the flying automobiles in *The Jetsons*. They envisioned the future from the point of view of a past that is by now totally anachronistic.'[69] The pop group Devo donned identical grey suits and ziggurat-like 'energy domes', their quotation of 1950s science fiction and Cold War paranoia, even performing glowing as if radioactive; they suggested not evolution but its opposite, an unwinding of the past or de-evolution.

Kate Pierson, Fred Schneider, Keith Strickland, Cindy Wilson and Ricky Wilson of The B-52s, 1980.

Sotheby's promotion of the Chantal jukebox in 1973 may have been premature: by the mid-1980s a flood of kidney-shaped couches, tapas bars with pink and blue organic furnishings and gaudy Hawai'ian shirts

Devo's Robert Mothersbaugh, wearing the band's trademark red hat, 1979.

decorated with rocket ships recalled the futuristic Modernism of the 1950s more than the rock 'n' roll revival, shifting the character of the revival from teenage rebellion to middle-class aspiration. But Philco's Predicta line of television sets of 1958, prized by collectors in the 1980s, were actually a market failure when originally introduced; the period's Modernistic futurism was but one of a plethora of 1950s styles, affording consumers wide choice. But the revival of the period's Modernism affirmed concerns in the 1970s and '80s, as much as the 1950s.

When Ronald Reagan came into office in 1981, some commentators tried to link his politics with the 1950s revival; comparing Reagan to

Dwight Eisenhower, Lance Morrow of *Time* suggested that he represented 'a militant nostalgia, a will almost to veto the intervening years and start again on earlier premises'.[70] But retro is not nostalgia. As Richard Horn noted in *Fifties Style: Then and Now* (1985), 1950s retro expressed 'a certain cynicism, wearing '50s-style clothes in the 1980s can be interpreted as a kind of social protest in and of itself'.[71] Jed Perl discerned two forms of 1950s recall: 'Treated reverently,' he noted, "'50s style can suggest second thoughts about the youth revolt of the '60s. Treated irreverently, the same design elements are an announcement that the insurrection is alive and well. You don't have to like Ike in order to appreciate the lightness, the friendly irony, of '50s design.'[72] It may be, as Horn insisted in 1985, that

> many people – especially those under thirty – are not overly optimistic about the future . . . nuclear nightmares haunted the popular imagination of the 1950s. Today they strike many people as a possible daytime threat – a reality rather than a dream. And it is no wonder that fashionable young people don clothes recalling an era of nuclear naïveté with a decidedly ironic air.[73]

But the older period was hardly naive. Nelson's Ball Clocks and the bikini swimsuit tried to come to terms with nuclear realities as much as duck-and-cover drills and bomb shelters. By the 1980s the nuclear threat had not vanished; the militarization of space and the development of long-range missiles revived nuclear fears. It was post-war efforts to normalize the nuclear threat and still look optimistically towards the future that struck observers three decades later as naive.

The idea of post-war revival drew the French *mode rétro* into the orbit of the 1950s revival. True to retro's grab-bag approach to history, as both revivals were popularized, their historical boundaries began to blur. In the 1970s fashion press, retro became a byword for clothes that quoted both the French 1940s and the American 1950s. Nevertheless, alluding to invasion and collaboration, the French *mode rétro* carried different associations from the technological hopes and fears of the American post-war years. At their most incisive, both revivals attempted to rediscover and confront the past through immersion in it. But the 1950s revival did not only question the past, it also appraised the past's view of the future. Immersion in the 1950s past also meant coming to terms with its culture of technological optimism and discovering that the future is not what it used to be.

CHAPTER FOUR

The Lure of Yesterday's Tomorrows

In the early 1980s the American graphic designer Paula Scher was shocked to find 'a couple of terrific El Lissitzky and Alexander Rodchenko posters' within the pages of her 'moldy art history books'.[1] After years of routinely flipping past Russian Constructivist images Scher admitted that she ignored them when she was 'ripping off Art Nouveau and Art Deco designs'. In 1974 she was taken aback when she took note of an iconic poster of 1929 by Lissitzky for the Kunstgewerbemuseum in Zurich, which fused the heads of a young man and woman with photomontage and stamped their brow with the initials USSR. At that time she 'looked at the giant USSR foreheads and said, "Too weird"'.[2] By 1979, however, Lissitzky and his Russian contemporaries carried new cachet. Scher admitted that she had been influenced by a wave of books and museum shows devoted to early Russian Modernist art. Moreover, she acknowledged, 'it was also no coincidence that many of my designer friends had gone "Russian crazy" at the same time. When 500 unrelated people say "That's great!" at the same time and incorporate the influence into their work, it constitutes a movement.'[3]

Bristling with a visionary fervour that made other styles appear quaint and impoverished, avant-garde art of the early twentieth century underwent a series of re-evaluations in the 1960s and '70s. But the art and design from the Bolshevik Revolution of 1917 remained the biggest rediscovery; it had been long suppressed within the Soviet Union and avoided in the West for its Communist associations. Nevertheless, the post-Stalinist thaw of the 1960s and early 1970s saw aspects of Russian Constructivism and Suprematism appear throughout the West. For left-leaning artists and intellectuals, this art hovered on a hopeful horizon, ratifying a set of utopian social goals that seemed to have disappeared from both politics and art. The resurrection of early Modernism in the 1970s began as a high-minded affair, but its idiom was quickly transformed, becoming less a gesture of solidarity than a mark of hip taste. Moreover, as the modern past was revisited, observers noticed that the future was also changing.

Warming Up the Cold War

The high point of Richard Nixon's policy of détente with the Soviet Union may have been the signing of the Strategic Arms Limitation Treaty in 1972, but this diplomatic effort had an unexpected benefit – an abundance of Russian art made its way West. In the rush to reduce political tension, cultural exchanges were an obvious extension of public policy. What had begun as a westward trickle of Russian Revolution-era art during the 1960s became a flood by the 1970s. Although the Soviet government remained highly ambivalent about these works, the numerous artists and designers living in the West had no such qualms. During a politically confused decade, they saw in the visual language pioneered by Rodchenko, Lissitzky and others a syntax of rebellion.

By the 1960s many early twentieth-century art movements received renewed attention; Robert Motherwell's *Dada Painters and Poets* of 1951, for instance, was especially important in repositioning Dada as a major influence on twentieth-century art. Conversely, on the fiftieth anniversary of the founding of the Weimar Bauhaus in 1968, the West German government supported a massive retrospective show, *50 Jahre Bauhaus*. Bolstered by the nation's self-confidence in its pre-Nazi past, the exhibition stimulated re-evaluations of the Bauhaus legacy, and prompted James Mellow to remark in the *New York Times* that its designs 'look as modern today as they did when they were created several decades ago'.[4]

The resurgence of interest in Constructivism and Suprematism was, by contrast, a furtive phenomenon. Where the West German government heavily promoted Bauhaus accomplishments, the Soviet leadership remained deeply conflicted over its artistic past. During the Revolution, Russia's artistic avant-garde had adapted aspects of European vanguard art, including Cubism and Futurism, to express radical political and economic ideals. Hoping to redesign society itself, leading artists and designers sought to fuse aesthetics with industrial production; their austere geometry and red-and-black palette provided visual direction to a world trembling on the brink of philosophical and social disaster.

Nevertheless, such art was soon impinged by ideological shifts within the Communist Party. Under Stalin, major initiatives for change in the late 1920s and early 1930s led the authorities to steer Russia's avant-garde away from abstraction and foreign influences. By 1932 individual artistic groups were disbanded and replaced by Party-led unions. From wholesome illustrations of peasant folk tales to heroic depictions of Russian leaders, the government began to promote a style of Socialist Realist art that politicians believed would resonate with the masses. Russian art history passed over the revolutionary era in chagrined silence. The official *History of Russian Art* (1955) squeezed the years 1917–24 into its twelfth volume, mainly to identify non-objective art with enemies of the Soviet state.[5] Artists and writers associated with the revolutionary vanguard fared poorly. Luckier than many, Vladimir Tatlin died in obscurity in Moscow in 1953. Having fashioned himself as a proletarian theorist in the 1920s, the poet, critic and graphic artist Vladimir Mayakovsky was deeply distressed by later criticism that his work was formalist and elitist; he shot himself in 1930. Nikolai Punin, a critic, theorist and art historian critical of later developments and supportive of artists like Tatlin, was arrested on no charges and sent to a prison camp near the Arctic Circle, where he died in 1948.

In the West, subtleties of ideology mattered little. While the Soviet avant-garde had been widely exhibited in the 1920s, it slipped off the radar by the 1950s. At the height of the Cold War, art from the Russian Revolution was avoided for its Communist associations; the historian Paul Wood described Western ideas of Russia as an 'intellectual dark continent, probed, if at all, by hostile Kremlinologists rather than sympathetic students of a vivid cultural constellation'.[6] Even standard surveys such as Reyner Banham's *Theory and Design in the First Machine Age* (1960) barely touched the Russian contribution to early Modernism.

Stalin's death in 1953, though, inaugurated a new era in Soviet cultural politics. While official censure of revolutionary art continued, the older period was quietly re-evaluated by Soviet intellectuals, themselves nostalgic for the early promise of the Revolution. Private exhibitions of Russian art from the early twentieth century were held in academies and scientific institutions; the elite Kurchatov Institute of Atomic Energy in Moscow, for instance, held small, unpublicized shows of works by Ivan Kliun, Mikhail Larionov and Liubov Popova. In official organs like *Sovetskaya kultura*, a newspaper published by the Ministry of Culture, leading critics began to call for official reappraisal of these earlier styles.

The West was also paying attention. With this post-Stalin thaw, scholars like Camilla Gray, whose *The Great Experiment: Russian Art, 1863–1922* was published in 1962, gained access to Soviet collections and reintroduced Russia's early Modernism to the West. The work of Lissitzky, Kazimir Malevich, Rodchenko and Tatlin provided natural inspiration for Minimalist art. In the early 1960s, artists like Carl Andre and Dan Flavin were influenced by Russian art, the latter even producing a series of 'monuments' to Tatlin beginning in 1964. Indeed, the Russian avant-garde was quickly canonized; Western intellectuals and artists regarded the older period, as the critic Hilton Kramer noted in 1971, with 'an almost religious veneration. Malevich, Tatlin, Rodchenko, Lissitzky, and Popova are (among others) the saints of this new aesthetic faith.'[7]

Nixon's policy of détente was well timed to fuel the 1960s resurrection of Russian revolutionary art. Beginning in 1969, Leonid Brezhnev and Nixon began serious discussions to limit the proliferation of strategic arms. While most diplomats and politicians focused on détente's implications for foreign policy, some museum curators clamoured for access to Russian Suprematist and Constructivist works, still little known in the West. However, Soviet culture ministers faced a bind. Eager to gain cultural prestige abroad, they did not want to rankle bureaucrats at home; Russia's early Modernists remained politically suspect. Even Russian state galleries were not permitted to exhibit their substantial collections of art by the Revolution's avant-garde. This conflict haunted Western exhibitions of Russian art in the late 1960s and early 1970s. In 1971 the Hayward Gallery in London offered two different exhibition catalogues in conjunction with *Art in Revolution: Soviet Art and Design since 1917*. One catalogue, published with a striking red, black and white cover, numerous illustrations and what the *New York Times* called 'informative, enthusiastic essays', celebrated the art of the Russian Revolution.[8] The other catalogue, with a sober black-and-white cover and a single introductory essay by an official Soviet art historian, was shaped by the Soviet Ministry of Culture. Moreover, shortly before the show opened, officials from the Soviet embassy were surprised to find an entire room devoted to works by Lissitzky that were proscribed by the current government. Too late to change, the space was boarded up and painted over; other works by Lissitzky, Malevich and Popova were judged as having 'not much contact with the masses', and removed individually as well.[9]

Such conflict hardly tarnished the reputations of the artists being exhibited; instead it simply added to the art's defiant allure. Kramer spoke for some, calling Russia's early Modernism a 'utopian swindle' that provided a dismal 'ideal model of what the art of the future must encompass'.[10] Others, like the graphic designer Paula Scher, saw the Russian avant-garde as an answer to 'a period of negativity, conservatism, and a general lowering of our personal and economic expectations. Constructivist work could make us feel we were creating a visual rebellion in inspired times.'[11] By the 1970s the art of the Russian Revolution, like much of early Modernism, struck many artists and intellectuals as a utopian path not taken.

As the West entered a period of economic and social malaise in the early 1970s, Constructivism and Suprematism held a sternly seductive

David King, poster for
Apartheid in Practice, 1978.

Neville Brody, Red
Wedge logo, 1985.

appeal. In the United States, the Watergate scandal, the Vietnam War and an economy suddenly in thrall to OPEC brought on a national crisis of confidence. Britain's ready affluence of the 1960s left a heavy hangover; experiencing its worst unemployment since World War Two, the nation seemed to be on an ever-accelerating decline. In 1975 the British Chancellor of the Exchequer, Denis Healey, planned to cut public expenditure by £3 billion and the ranks of the jobless reached 1.5 million. As capitalism flagged, imagery from the Russian Revolution was boldly aloof, brimming with ideological and aesthetic self-assurance. While Soviet culture ministers were ambivalent about the art and design from their own revolution, its visionary promise filtered into museum exhibitions around the world; reviewing one such show in 1981, Peter Schjeldahl averred:

> whatever else the Russians did, *they lived* [italics his]. Day by day, they articulated a world on the turn by acting on and being acted on by it . . . I'm at a loss for how to start applying all this to our

mazy current straits. Just think of it as a call for a newly mobilized dissatisfaction.[12]

Others too looked for ways to apply the utopian idealism of Russia's early Modernism in the 1970s. On the British Left, grace notes from psychedelia appeared in underground publications while grassroots movements like the Campaign for Nuclear Disarmament (CND) relied on simple signage and slogans inspired by the Modernist clarity. As the designer David King would later note, 'there wasn't a visual style on the Left – it was a mishmash'.[13] After a research trip to Moscow in 1970, King, then art director for the *Sunday Times* magazine, began designing increasingly Suprematist-inflected pieces not only for the magazine, but also for books and catalogues of post-détente exhibitions like the Hayward Gallery's *Art in Revolution*. A self-described 'nonaligned Leftist',[14] King was joined by designers like Richard Hollis, who employed a Russian-inflected design vocabulary in his poster for the Lissitzky exhibition of 1977 at the Museum of Modern Art in Oxford, to evoke the earlier period's austerity. While King would later argue that he did not consciously make his work 'look Russian',[15] the simple, emphatic elements of his later designs for organizations like Apartheid in Practice (1978), the Anti-Nazi-League and the National Union of Journalists bear an unmistakable debt to Russian revolutionary art. By the early 1980s this political vocabulary was increasingly associated with Britain's mainstream Left. Neville Brody's logo for Red Wedge, a British music industry collective of rock musicians in favour of the Labour Party, owed a singular debt to Lissitzky's poster of 1919, *Beat the Whites with the Red Wedge*.

But elsewhere this political message was increasingly lost as early Modernism and Russian revolutionary art was assimilated into Britain's burgeoning punk subculture as one of a series of stylistic gestures. From fanzines to bondage pants, handbills to record album covers, punk's youthful anti-authoritarianism translated into a 'Do-It-Yourself', or DIY, design vocabulary.[16] Some of the most ambitious figures in punk, such as Malcolm McLaren and Jamie Reid, sought to subvert a burgeoning commodity culture and its advertising by adopting the rhetoric of the Frenchman Guy Debord and the Situationist International, while many others turned to ransacking the rich heritage of early twentieth-century Modernism. When Reid, from the *Suburban Press*, was enlisted by McLaren to help shape the visual image of the band the Sex Pistols, he 'saw punk as part of an art movement that's gone over the last hundred years, with roots in Russian agitprop, Surrealism, Dada and Situationism'.[17]

Russia's revolutionary art, as well as a host of other forms from early Modernism, appeared in punk subculture, especially its albums. While enthusiastically co-opting imagery from the past, the punk approach suggested industrial nihilism rather than the allusive eclecticism of the Art Nouveau and Art Deco revivals. Designers like Barney Bubbles, born Colin Fulcher, emerged in the mid-1970s with a graphic language indebted to the more rebellious tendrils of early Modernism. His cover for *Music for Pleasure* (1977) by The Damned owes a clear if attenuated debt to numerous Modern movements, from the brilliantly saturated geometry of Vasily Kandinsky to Joan Miró's biomorphic austerity. Russia's early Modernism was especially influential. Designers were enamoured by its heady rebelliousness; Al McDowell soon established the design firm Rocking Russian, its name inspired by Bubbles' cover designs.

British designers working in the music industry were hardly alone in rediscovering and reconfiguring Constructivist work. The album *Man Machine* (1978) by the German band Kraftwerk is a pioneering work in electronic sound and precursor to house, ambient and techno styles, featuring a severe red-and-black cover whose harsh, angular typefaces and regimented group portrait were humorously credited to Lissitzky. Kraftwerk's electronically distorted vocals and robotically thumping synthesizers evoke a post-industrial world apart from the ferocity of punk rock. Its hypnotically sterile sound and austere machine imagery lifted from the Russians

Kraftwerk, album cover for *Man Machine,* 1978.

evoke less the factory floor idealism of Russia's revolutionary avant-garde than a compelling, if somewhat chilling, vision of the world in which musical ecstasy is rendered cool, mechanical and precise.

Even when transfigured, many in the mainstream found Russia's earnestly intense aesthetics too extreme. When Brody was asked to redesign the neo-Constructivist look of the left-leaning London entertainment guide *City Limits* in the early 1980s, he observed that people were given the choice 'take it or leave it', and there was no possible chance of subversion, no chance to reaching the wider public who might buy *City Limits* because they simply wanted to go out and enjoy themselves . . . it had the effect of a black cloud, and for someone looking for entertainment it looked depressing.[18]

It was only with the advent of the retro design movement, and its light-hearted revisiting of early Modernist graphic design, that such imagery jumped the cultural fire line and became seductively appealing to the broader buying public.

'Jive Modernism' and the Women Who Saved New York

By the mid-1980s Switzerland's venerable watch industry was over-whelmed by Asian competitors; with its international market share falling from 30 per cent in 1974 to half that by 1984, Swiss banks forced the merger of the country's two largest watchmakers in 1983. The Swiss also changed tactics: they created a new watch. Cheap, sturdy, analogue and designed to reach buyers at an 'emotional' level, the Swatch watch stunned industry analysts. As an inexpensive, well-manufactured product of a high-wage country, the Swatch challenged established economic wisdom. Marketed with the motto 'high Swiss [and] low cost', it also contradicted perceptions of 'stateless' multinational companies. As one executive insisted, Swatch was convinced that its products would appeal to 'a sympathetic audience . . . Europeans and Americans are damn happy if you can show that their societies are not decadent.'[19] As early as 1984, a Bloomingdales buyer breathlessly reported that customers came to the store to 'buy two, three, even five at a time'.[20] By 1985 the company earned $200 million in sales of watches and related products.

The Swiss employed several significant business strategies, but crucial among them was what Swatch executives called 'a complete communications programme' that employed advertising with strikingly retro imagery. The distinctly Swiss Modernist overtones of Swatch's American ad campaign of 1985 helped to draw consumers away from Asian competition. In Zurich, Swatch's rapid ascendance was greeted with relief and heralded a new way of approaching production. In New York, its advertising campaign was heralded as part of a broader retro movement that would save the city's status as America's pre-eminent advertising centre. Still, many in design circles would soon complain about its free use of older imagery, asserting that it signified the advent of 'jive Modernism'. First identified by the critic and historian Philip Meggs,[21] graphic design's retro movement was initially limited to Scher, Louise Fili, Carin Goldberg and Lorraine Louie; from spidery Art Nouveau lettering to sleek sans-serif fonts inspired by the Bauhaus, these retro designers each made use of the typefaces, compositional strategies and imagery of early Modernism. Each mixed unconventional typefaces in boldly geometric configurations. Unusual in late 1970s design, they frequently emphasized typography over illustration. More importantly, their pillaging of art's Modern past was accessible to the general public.

Working in the relatively conservative publishing and entertainment industries, these innovative designers were all female. Certainly retro was only one approach they used, but beginning with Scher's work for CBS Records in the late 1970s, it became a widely recognized and distinctive style. Her album poster *Best of Jazz* (1979) featured Constructivist-inspired type placed at 45-degree angles and a palette of red, white and black. But the Russian avant-garde was not the only Modernist design vocabulary that fuelled retro. Goldberg recycled the spindly lettering of the Viennese Secessionist Josef Hoffmann for a book jacket of Rainer Maria Rilke's *Sonnets to Orpheus* (1985). Alternately, Fili's cover design of 1983 for Marguerite Duras's novel *The Lover* cultivated a consciously low-key historicist approach, coupling outmoded 1930s typefaces with a delicate rose palette. The most

notorious example of historical recycling, however, was Scher's poster of
1986 for Swatch. Based on Herbert Matter's iconic poster of 1934 for the Swiss
Tourist Bureau, itself a photomontage inspired by Lissitzky, the Swatch ad
clearly tapped older design traditions. Scher replaced the original's tightly
kerned 'SCHWEIZ' tagline with a loosely kerned 'SWATCH'. The designer
also added a hand and wrist wrapped with three Swatch watches in the lower
right corner; company executives later insisted they be enlarged from her
original sketch, a familiar refrain echoed in the title of Scher's autobiographical book *Make It Bigger* (2002). Despite, or perhaps because of, such
compromises, the Swatch image stood out from mainstream advertising.

In Meggs's *Print* magazine article of 1989, 'The Women Who Saved
New York', he characterized Fili, Goldberg, Louie and Scher as 'a new and
unexpected movement'. By revitalizing a somewhat moribund Madison

Louise Fili, cover for Marguerite
Duras, *The Lover* (1983).

Avenue, he argued, they were poised to salvage the city's floundering advertising reputation.[22] Ironically, none of the group was affiliated with the
city's major advertising firms. Madison Avenue's highly touted agencies,
meanwhile, were hardly the bearded emissaries who had promoted the
counter-cultural 'Creative Revolution' some twenty years earlier. Although
their firms now offered a full range of professional services, including
public relations, corporate identity and even product design, industry
observers and clients alike complained that the dominant agencies were
becoming wheezy, unresponsive and, perhaps most damning, producing
unimaginative advertising. Smaller, more nimble 'boutique' agencies flourished in cities like Minneapolis, Portland and San Francisco, and in 1988
the momentum was undeniable when Minneapolis agencies were awarded
twice as many of the advertising industry's prestigious CLIO awards for
print campaigns than New York firms.

Paula Scher, advertisement for Swatch watch, 1985.

Retro's engagement with early Modernism seemed especially fresh in an industry where, as Jeff Goodby of the San Francisco advertising agency Goodby, Berlin & Silverstein insisted, 'the rules are gone'.[23] Blending, reshuffling and transforming sources as varied as marquees from London cinemas and Piet Mondrian's *Broadway Boogie-Woogie* (1942–3) provided cheap and accessible imagery for youth-oriented industries with slim design budgets and even slimmer expectations; as Scher admitted in 1984, 'the wonderful thing about being a designer in the music business is that nothing has to mean anything'.[24] Moreover, like Scher, many retro designers worked for the recording industry where the success of Britain's independent labels was well noted by the late 1970s. Still, punk design remained too extreme for top-selling CBS recording artists, and few decision-makers appreciated or recognized even early Modernist associations. Executives at the corporate offices of CBS in New York, for instance, balked when Scher introduced Russian-inspired designs, claiming that they 'didn't look serious enough'.[25] Of her Constructivist-inspired *Best of Jazz* poster, Scher noted that

> the design had far more to do with the necessity of fitting names into a given space (the economy was bad and the budget was thin) than with any desire to return to the principles of the Russian avant-garde. I had always used style pragmatically. I found that in the '80s, among both clients and practitioners, circumstance was forgotten and style was an end in itself.[26]

Depoliticized, such imagery was reinvented for the 1980s. As the president of a consumer-marketing firm observed in 1991, 'newness used to have a cachet all by itself. It doesn't anymore.'[27] The popular press, meanwhile, began to perceive nostalgia as ubiquitous, hailing retro as a defining sensibility of the mid-1980s. The *Guardian* pronounced 'retro mania' as the principle design trend in 1987,[28] and even the starchy *Christian Science*

Monitor pronounced 'retro-chic' as a 'big trend' in the same year.[29] For some, the term retro was linked with anything even faintly nostalgic. But, much of retro's imagery drew from early Modernism. From shampoo packaged in Mondrian-esque squares of primary colours to the uncredited use of Lissitzky's work on an Arthur Andersen accounting firm brochure, the language of early Modernism became the language of sales.[30]

Perhaps the strangest journey was made by the imagery from the Russian Revolution. The early utopian promise that resurfaced in the West in the 1970s was altered; just as *glasnost* began to allow greater personal freedom in the Soviet Union, the art of its revolutionary avant-garde became part of the capitalist retro revival. Describing the phenomenon in 1987, the design writer Rick Poynor noted: 'the red and the black is not just back, it's everywhere about us. From the catwalks of Paris to design group letterheads, and from trendy T-shirts with Soviet slogans to the Suprematist teacups on sale at Oggetti, it's hip to think Red Square.'[31] Surveying the style's new-found and increasingly apolitical popularity, the historian Paul Wood facetiously remarked in 1992 that 'the most dangerous rumor concerning the Russian avant-garde has to do with its alleged support of radical politics, and radical political philosophy in general'.[32] The reuse of imagery from the Russian Revolution created a disconnect between marketing contrivance and historical content. Poyner alleged that: 'drained of their ideological content, the devices and motifs of Russian revolutionary art have been reduced to a *style* [italics his]'.[33] Even earlier, Baudrillard had argued against 'a retro politics, emptied of substance and legalized in their superficial exercise, with the air of a game and a field of adventure'. Although Baudrillard was not thinking of shampoo and T-shirts, his warning of retro's role in the age of simulacra reverberates through such arguments.[34]

Highly lucrative for image-conscious firms, retro style was also increasingly criticized from within the art community, and its empty evocation of early twentieth-century utopias was dubbed 'jive modernism'.

When a sour, off-key version of the Beatles' 'Yesterday' opened the keynote address of the designer Tibor Kalman at the 'Modernism and Eclecticism' symposium of 1990 at New York's School for Visual Arts, retro became a battleground in the culture wars. Kalman, who positioned himself as a provocateur while working for Benetton, *Interview* and the Times Square Redevelopment Project in New York throughout the late 1980s, castigated the recycling of older styles. Later, in the *Print* magazine article 'Good History, Bad History', Kalman, J. Abbott Miller and Carrie Jacobs announced that 'the '80s were a decade of comebacks: suspenders, miniskirts, Roy Orbison, Sugar Ray Leonard . . . But the really big comeback was history. We got rid of history in the '60s; saw what the world looked like without it in the '70s; and begged it to come back in the '80s. And it did; it came back with a vengeance.'[35] Scher's Swatch poster was singled out because it 'self-consciously mimics the Herbert Matter poster, not merely uses it as a point of departure. This is a familiar strategy (see Duchamp's Mona Lisa). However, the contextual displacement effected from Swiss tourism to Swatch watches is not particularly thought-provoking.'[36] Reflective cultural referencing, however, was not Swatch's goal; as the *New York Times* noted in 1987, 'ever since the first Swatch watches hit American shores in the fall of 1983, it has seemed as though every offbeat thing the company did turned out right'.[37] Scher herself would later claim the poster as a form of joking parody of its source.[38]

The arguments swirling around retro design inevitably included Postmodernism, the intellectual movement that rejected Modernism's transcendent individualism, while enjoying almost unrivalled currency in academic and artistic circles during the 1980s. The larger literary and theoretical apparatus that girded this intellectual movement encompassed the work of Sherrie Levine, Richard Prince and Mike Bidlo, who garnered critical attention for their challenge to accepted ideas of authorship and originality. Often without official permission or legal authority, artists in the 1980s used appropriation to tap early Modernist works; Levine, for instance, photographed iconic images by Mondrian, Vincent Van Gogh and Edward Weston.

When Scher's Swatch ad was published in *Mademoiselle*, however, it differed in both intent and context from the Levine photographs mounted at the Paula Cooper Gallery in New York. With corporate legal concerns ever a priority, the practical boundaries for appropriation in design remained more sharply delineated than in gallery art; where many appropriations were unhindered by issues like copyright, Scher conscientiously obtained legal permission to use Matter's image from his widow. Moreover, near the model's grinning face, Scher's version added a hand and wrist strapped with two Swatch watches, riffing on the history of graphic design but also making its commercial purpose plain.

Such recycling was on a collision course with an increasingly critically oriented design profession, highlighting not only the field's awkward position between commerce and art but also the larger relevance and treatment of history. Scher's use of Matter's photomontage was a far more volatile strategy than the recycled Beardsley drawings, or Art Deco borders of a generation earlier; while these forms remained an equivocal part of the Modernist legacy, purists objected to the treatment of work by recent figures as 'if it were something that was thought up by the ancient Romans, something dead from long ago'.[39] Even more important, it implicitly questioned Modernism's claim on contemporaneity. Traditionally, Modernity had been seen as a destination, rather than a way station that had been passed by, returnable to only through revival. The work of Modernist artists, architects and designers was intended to be timeless and morally uplifting. When Paul Rand, the acknowledged dean of American design, assessed Matter's career in 1978 he insisted that his work 'has that timeless, unerring quality one recognizes instinctively'.[40] While relatively few of Swatch's millions of customers would have recognized Matter's iconic imagery or Scher's reuse of it, many appreciated its slightly ironic optimism and vague reference to pre-war advertising. Certainly, Modernism's reputation never declined in the manner of the earlier Art Deco and Art Nouveau movements. But few notices of its death could be more effective than its ultimate recycling in a revival. To Kalman and his colleagues, 'Modernism failed because the spirit of it, the optimism, was lost'.[41] Indeed, Rand had argued that Matter's work was both 'commercial' and 'contemplative', enhancing 'the quality of life'.[42] As Kalman argued with other designers, 'what we can learn from Constructivism is not type placed at 45-degree angles and the reduction of colors to red, white, and black, but freedom with word order and the lack of strict hierarchies in the typographical message . . . we should focus not on its stylistic iterations but on its ideas'.[43] Few attended the call issued by Kalman, however, who ended his diatribe against retro, asking 'Now what can *you* do [italics his]?' For many in and outside the design community, the advent of retro suggested not only an optimism that was lost, but it also signalled that a certain way of seeing the future was also past.

Retro-futurism

'The future is not what it used to be', or so claimed anonymous graffiti in the early 1970s.[44] Conceptions of the future, as much as the Modernist past, began to be reconfigured in the 1970s. The popular culture of the 1960s and '70s saw a retrenchment that transfigured nostalgia into retro, while remaining strikingly unconcerned with fixing the problems of the present. But uncertainty about the future also began to be expressed by scholars and public alike. Above all, the optimistic visions of the future that defined previous generations began to disappear; instead, many hankered after yesterday's tomorrows. Retro nostalgia hankered for a world of flying cars and plastic houses. The oxymoron retro-futurism, the discrepancy between what the future once represented and what it no longer means, seeped into popular and academic culture in the 1970s. In the 1960s Art Nouveau and

Art Deco grew a patina of acquired significance; early Modernism was simi-larly transformed in the 1970s. As the theologian Martin E. Marty commented in 1975, 'the past is back in favor because the present is too unattractive to provide a base for looking with hope into the future'.[45]

Since the Renaissance, speculative optimism had focused on the disci-plined morality of utopia. By the nineteenth century, however, extended studies of history, as well as the advent of Darwinism, encouraged tentative visions of the future. As industrialization assaulted society with constant change, technological developments encouraged optimistic imaginings, like the submarines and propeller-powered balloons of Jules Verne. From Le Corbusier's vision of cities filled with shimmering skyscrapers to Lissitzky's sleek photomontages of Soviet factories, vanguard artists and designers of the early twentieth century also embraced a technical alchemy that would transfigure societies with applied science and industrial might. Popular culture, too, welcomed a better life achieved through technologi-cal change. Magazines like *Science Wonder Stories* and *Future Science Fiction* envisioned new ways of living that would captivate the most ardent machine buffs. By the time Monsanto Chemical Company opened 'The House of the Future' (1957) at Disneyland's Tomorrowland, many visitors anticipated a future resonant with Disney's slogan, 'if you can dream it, you can do it'. Fuelled by the US–Soviet space race and the advent of new mate-rials like plastics, such optimistic prognostication continued well into the 1960s. Beneath this enthusiasm, however, the shiny futurism of previous decades had begun to tarnish.

Paradoxically, retro-futurism took shape in the 1970s, a period charac-terized by rapid and intense technological progress. From the introduction of the microprocessor to the jumbo jet, the neutron bomb to the test-tube baby, applied science flourished. Yet many in the general public began to question whether technology could be an agent of social justice. Behind the utopian implications of forward-looking science lurked tales of woe, including the defilement of the natural environment and the depletion of

Monsanto House of the Future, Disneyland, Anaheim, California, c. 1957.

energy resources. The French theological philosopher Jacques Ellul, whose *The Technological Society* was first published in France in 1954 and appeared in the United States ten years later, anticipated the widespread disenchantment, while Alvin Toffler's best-selling *Future Shock* of 1970 predicted that people would soon be driven mad by technological change. Public wariness of applied science was undeniable.

Moreover, real technological achievement was disillusioning, even disempowering. Although man had landed on the moon, daily life remained banal. Technological spin-offs from the American space programme from medical equipment to new forms of insulation were real, but they lacked the dazzle that earlier visions of the future had promised. As doubts about the role of technology increased, plans made in the thrall of bygone, more alluring visions of the future were themselves derailed. Throughout the 1970s NASA programmes were scaled back and American plans to construct a civil transport faster than the speed of sound were quashed. There was an increased call from environmentalists for 'appropriate technology', while less glamorous but more economical human, wind- or solar-powered energy systems like wind turbines and solar panels were infused with new vigour and a pressing morality. Exuberant technological optimism lingered in fewer and fewer popular outposts, relegated largely to the pages of *Popular Science* or *Popular Mechanics*.

For some this 'crisis of confidence' proved a new source of inspiration. By the late 1970s and early 1980s science fiction pervaded culture in a new way; it was studied seriously for the first time, its history becoming a staple of university classes and publishing alike. Books such as Paul Carter's *The Creation of Tomorrow: Fifty Years of Magazine Science Fiction* (1977) and Tim Onosko's *Wasn't the Future Wonderful?* (1979) looked back almost enviously at the crystalline cities, space stations and starships that had packed science fiction between the wars. Others, for instance, *Fantastic Science-Fiction Art, 1926–1954* (1975) by Lester Del Rey, *Alternate Worlds: The Illustrated History of Science Fiction* (1975) by James Gunn, and *Science Fiction Art: The Fantasies of SF* (1975) compiled by Brian Aldiss, highlighted the starry-eyed and outright bizarre images that had drawn many readers to science fiction in the first place.

Alternately elegiac and parodic, 1970s visions of the future also looked backwards. George Lucas made *Star Wars* (1977) only after he failed to secure the rights for a remake of *Buck Rogers* or *Flash Gordon*. Indeed, Lucas's earlier *THX 1138* (1971) opened with a *Buck Rogers* trailer of 1939, then shifted scene to the twenty-fifth century. A triumph of Modernist design with strikingly bleak and Minimalist sets, the film was as forbiddingly dystopic as *Buck Rogers* was bracingly optimistic. *Star Wars*, meanwhile, melded past and future with wistful cheer, splicing lumbering space stations and twirling laser battles with visual quotes from the 1930s

C-3PO from *Star Wars*, 1977.

and '40s. The metallic anthropod C-3PO, for instance, recalls the female robot of Fritz Lang's *Metropolis* (1927), as well as Elektro, the friendly man-machine at Westinghouse's World's Fair exhibit of 1939–40. A gritty *mélange* of transfigured 1940s fashions and Art Deco buildings provided the backdrop for Ridley Scott's noirish and highly influential *Blade Runner* (1982), which set a template for films set in the future. Picturing Los Angeles *circa* 2019, the movie marquees and ziggurat-shaped buildings of the 1930s suggested that the past would never fade away; the future was increasingly seen as a palimpsest of incomplete reflections and partial disclosures.

The previous decade's fascination with Art Nouveau, which had originally fashioned itself 'the modern style', as well as with the 'flash and trash' aesthetic of Art Deco,[46] already suggested a nostalgia not for a dreamily romanticized past but rather for the buoyant futurism of the early

Kenny Scharf, *Ships*, 1979.

machine age. Roy Lichtenstein redesigned New York into a Buck Rogers landscape; Robert Smithson revelled in 'ultramoderne', a term more at home in the pages of *Astounding Science Fiction* of the 1930s than *Arts* magazine of the 1960s. Such Campy nostalgia for the past's visions of the future extended to early Modernism, with its hopeful projections of future utopias. The early optimism of Russian Constructivist art, for instance, held particular appeal to jaded tastes of the 1970s; seemingly anachronistic, its ebullient optimism was contagious. As Peter Plagens noted in an *Artforum* review of 1975, the art and design from the Russian Revolution contained 'such poignant faith in a brave new world, such innocent pleasure in the printing press' new gymnastics!' But he also lamented how this enthusiasm was poorly translated into contemporary art and design. Recalling the older period's fervour, he feared that 'when we try to recapture it ourselves, we end up with sequined boutique T-shirts of Chaplin, or Lichtenstein's

Peace Through Chemistry'.[47] Reviewing the 1970s use of Constructivist imagery, Scher would observe in 1984 that in 'our response to Russian Constructivism, I'm convinced that we're responding to our political and economic climate in both emotional and practical terms . . . The work of the Russian Constructivists represented the optimism of the Revolution and the Marxist utopian dream' and the future that it once promised.[48] For the electronic world of Kraftwerk, this translated into a sceptical optimism in the cold tech music and mechanical voices that echo the machine regimentation of their album cover after Lissitzky and their songs about robots and space labs, expressing a kind of post-industrial angst.

Not limited to early Modernism, by the late 1970s even the futurism of the more recent 1950s was nostalgically remembered in popular culture. The American pop group The B-52s took their name alternately from Southern slang for women's beehive hairstyles as well as the long-range bombers that entered US military service in 1954, while Kenny Scharf's glossy paintings like *Ships* (1979) fused space-age futurism with suburbia. As the architecture critic Nayana Currimbhoy recalled in 1987, 'in the '50s, technology was the magic carpet, ready to transport humankind into a bright new world'.[49] Renewed interest in Googie-style architecture was reinforced by preservationists seeking to save such post-war buildings for posterity. When the pop group Devo tapped memories of the Cold War and science fiction, it was with a tongue-in-cheek form of nostalgia.

In 1977 Paul Richard announced in the *Washington Post* that, just as 'the religion of the new is losing its adherents', a kind of 'Retro Art' was in ascendance. 'Future shock is fading', Richard continued, 'revolution slimming. Where artists used to prophesy, today they tend to quote. Retro Art is everywhere, in the antique flash of Star Wars, in the songs of Linda Ronstadt . . . Americans, it sometimes seems, have all become historians.'[50] Not only had the province of historians been colonized by non-professionals, but history's very relation to the present and future was also changing.

The switch from prophecy to quotation suggests a backward, rather than a forward orientation. When the public began asking not whether flying atomic cars or lunar cities were possible but rather whether they were even desirable, a form of progressivism intimately linked with ideas of Modernity was bygone, finished and truly over. Retro's highly self-conscious mix of derision and nostalgia provided a seductive ether, suggesting that history was something to be plundered rather than taken seriously. As Richard argued, the past 'has not been superseded. Instead, it's being mined'.[51] But it also posited a great divide, marking a cleaving away from the recent past; rather than forming a continuity, retro's nostal-gic mockery fuelled cultural narcissism. Retro's translation of recent history into consumable objects suggests how previous periods of popular culture and art and design can be used to characterize ourselves as distinct from the recent past.

Epilogue

In 1937, long before the rise of retro, the historian James Laver observed an easy fluidity linking a style's popular rejection and acceptance. Condensing these ideas, Laver wrote a breezy paradigm that predicted any new fashion's reception over a 160-year period. 'The same costume', he postulated,

> will be Indecent 10 years before its time, Shameless 5 years before its time, Outré (daring) 1 year before its time, Smart, Dowdy 1 year after its time, Hideous 10 years after its time, Ridiculous 20 years after its time, Amusing 30 years after its time, Quaint 50 years after its time, Charming 70 years after its time, Romantic 100 years after its time, Beautiful 150 years after its time.[1]

Dubbed 'Laver's Law', this timeline gives shape to fashionable change in the 'Modern' period, from the French Revolution to the early twentieth century. In tracing the evolving reception of a style from scandalous indecency to consecrated refinement, Laver's trajectory of taste implicitly emphasizes continuity. Retro, on the other hand, implies rupture.

Revelling in the outmoded and passé, retro claims a Camp sense of rediscovery. But retro also crosses an aesthetic threshold, replacing the 'Charming' and 'Romantic' with the 'Weird' and 'Ugly'.

In 1984, reflecting on her renewed interest in the iconic work of the early twentieth-century Russian revolutionary artist El Lissitzky, the graphic designer Paula Scher recalled how, some years earlier, she rejected Lissitzky's poster for the Zurich Kunstgewerbemuseum as 'too weird'. Five years later, seeing the poster a second time, she revised her opinion: now it was 'great'. Implicitly updating Laver's Law, Scher outlined her own retro-inflected timeframe for stylistic change. 'If we want to predict future graphic trends', she remarked,

> All we have to do is pick up poster books and tape record our responses to various genres and periods. Here's what the responses mean:
>
> 'That's Great' – What we are doing now, or will be doing tomorrow, even though every client will reject it.
>
> 'Nice' – What we have been doing for the past three years, and what we will resort to when 'That's Great' is rejected.
>
> 'Tired' – What we have been doing for the past five years.
>
> 'Too Weird' – What we will be doing in five years.
>
> 'Too Ugly' – What we will be doing in ten years.[2]

Where Laver's Law spans 160 years, Scher's time frame covers 15; if Laver outlines fashion's slow march towards historical acceptance, retro reaches the same end at an almost frantic pace. Retro does not allow historical epochs to grow old gracefully. Pulling a series of decade-based revivals through popular culture's hopper with predictable regularity, retro hastily transforms the 'Ugly' into the 'Great'. In so doing, retro privileges one aspect of Laver's Law, the 'Amusing'. Degrees of historical ripening and nuanced emotional reactions disappear; the 'Quaint', 'Charming', 'Romantic' and 'Beautiful' modes described by Laver vanish, replaced by the reflexive 'Weird' and 'Nice'. But retro's impact extends beyond graphic design. Acidic in its memorialization of the recent past, this tart-tongued form of revivalism has invaded our perception of history.

The recent past is increasingly understood in retro's sweepingly simple, often acerbic terms. In the 1980s the late 1960s were memorialized as a utopian hippie haven, reincarnated for eager consumers who bought paisley-patterned men's shirts and listened to psychedelic garage bands, followed by the latter-day space-warp of polystyrene bean bags and 'plastic fantastic' chairs, and televisions shaped like astronaut helmets. The 1970s have reappeared in Afro hairstyles and bell-bottoms, club disco nights evoking a freewheeling sexual fantasy to streetwise revivals of pre-commercial hip-hop music complete with T-shirts bearing pioneering rapper's portraits and reproductions of flyers for the first house parties. More recently, the 1980s have been resurrected, celebrated alternately for the cheery brightness of the period's pop culture, the remote techno-futurism of its electronically synthesized music and its emergent video-game culture. As one chronological revival inexorably follows another, retro transforms history's progress from a stately advance to a revolving door.

Retro revivalism views the past with trendy detachment. Encouraging Scher and others to rediscover early Modernism, the casual revivalism of the late 1970s and early 1980s occurred against a backdrop of Cold War thaw and economic and political malaise throughout the West. But where the Russian avant-garde originally crackled with prophetic enthusiasm, its retro reincarnation was less a gesture of socialist solidarity than a mark of hip taste. Writing in the same period, the French theorist Jean Baudrillard suggested that retro demythologizes the past. By analysing the role that history played in 1970s cinema, Baudrillard concluded that volatile issues of the past, for example Nazism, were now depicted ambiguously, without moral qualification. History was being drained of meaning. The reworking

Young man giving a 'victory' sign sports a 1970s retro look.

of early Modernism depoliticized its sources; by the mid-1980s, red and black graphics that recalled the Russian Revolution embellished accounting firms' advertising brochures. At best, retro recall revisits the past with acute ironic awareness; self-conscious in its recollection, retro revivalism lays bare the arbitrariness of historical memory. At its worst, retro pillages history with little regard for moral imperatives or nuanced implications. As entire periods of the recent past are introduced into the popular historical consciousness through retro's accelerated chronological blur, we risk incorporating its values as well.

Although chronologically close, retro posits a great divide separating the present from the recent past. In the nineteenth century, historical revivals built on past successes, using the past as a foundation that could be improved. Although we no longer cleave to the optimism of Modernism,

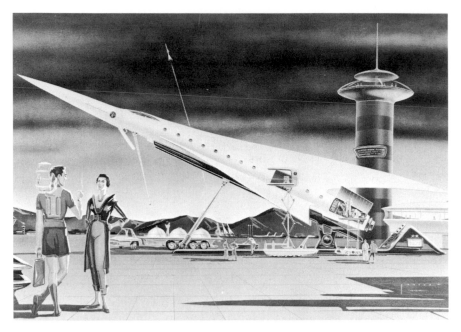

'Lunar Liner', c. 1958: an artist's impression of the future of space travel where tourists travel to and from the moon.

we have inherited the notion that everyday life is relentlessly changing. As a consequence, our experiences seem utterly different than what has passed before. The past, however recent, remains a remote and distinct Other. Retro recalls the past not only as separate, but also naive. It sardonically remembers when Elektro the robot drew a slack-faced crowd at Westinghouse's World's Fair exhibit of 1939–40 in New York and the casual futurism that imagined vacationers driving their tail-finned cars up to the lunar-liner airport. Deeming ourselves more sophisticated than previous generations, we have also outrun earlier forms of optimism; the future has become treacherous territory.

Retro distances us from the Modern past as we grapple with a haunting sense of not having lived up to its inheritance. When it opened in 1955,

Walt Disney's Tomorrowland promised a bright, clean and efficient world of plastic houses and flying cars. Its retro-inflected renovation in the late 1990s celebrates past visions of the future from Jules Verne and H. G. Wells to the World's Fair of 1939–40. Walt Disney's vision promised us lives of leisure and an escape from the mundane. Not only have those goals remained unfulfilled, but we also question whether the particulars of that vision are even desirable. Tomorrowland's PeopleMover, for instance, anticipated a future of efficient mass transit but was soon discovered to use more energy than any other exhibit in the park.[3] From energy worries to global warming, our concerns have shifted. But retro also echoes a sneaking suspicion that we have lost the optimistic confidence of earlier periods. According to Disney officials, Tomorrowland's renovation in 1998 mined the past because 'the dreams of the future are as appealing today as they were yesterday'.[4] Its irony tempered with a perverse form of longing, retro is almost reflexively defensive. As one Disney official remarked, 'It's harder for kids today to dream about living and taking a role in a future that's believable.'[5] Retro recall allows us to wall ourselves off from the recent past, positing a great divide separating it from the present. But it also admits a grudging fascination with the recent past.

When 'retro' rockets helped to popularize the term in the early 1960s, the term was closely linked to space-age technology. Essential for providing a counter thrust against the rocket's main momentum, the retro rockets were used at a vital moment to alter the spacecraft's course; without them the rocket would lose its trajectory or fail to decelerate properly for landing. Activated at a critical stage, the rockets provided a necessary boost backwards. Like these rockets, retro may look back but it also provides a final boost toward something new.

Janus-like, the retro past cannot be uncoupled from popular conceptions of the future. In the late 1960s and '70s, as fears of technology increased and many economies de-industrialized, the public's confidence in the future faltered. From telephones to television, the consumer products that heralded earlier technological breakthroughs survived, reminders of the technological leaps and bounds of an earlier age. Attention was focused on decline, from the gradual but persistent decrease of well-paying industrial jobs and the blight of closed factories, to lingering air and chemical pollution from waste fill and dumps. But much less consideration was given to what would come next. The past thirty years have experienced profound discoveries in science and technology, including advances in quantum and information sciences, bio- and nanotechnology. But these new innovations have done little to capture the popular imagination in the way that futurist magazines like *Amazing Stories* and *Mechanix Illustrated* vividly projected life-changing scientific advance during the inter-war years. Retro is a symptom, rather than an end; we are pulled to the past, because our visions of the future remain unformed.

References

Introduction: Remembering When We Were Modern

1 John Russell, 'London', *Art News*, LXV/52 (1966), p. 19.
2 Ibid.
3 A. D. Hippisley Coxe, 'Kinky Classics', *Design*, CLXXXVIII (1964), p. 66.
4 'New Look at Art Nouveau', *Time*, LXXXIV/52 (1964), p. 62.
5 Fredric Jameson, 'Nostalgia for the Present', *Postmodernism or the Cultural Logic of Late Capitalism* (Durham, NC, 1991), p. 283.
6 Bernardine Morris, 'Will the "Retro" Look Make It?', *New York Times* (1 January 1979), p. 18.
7 Lucy Lippard, 'Hot Potatoes: Art and Politics in 1980', in *Get the Message?: A Decade of Art for Social Change* (New York, 1984), p. 165.
8 Lucy Lippard, 'Rejecting Retrochic', in ibid., p. 176.
9 Lucy Lippard, 'Retrochic, Looking Back in Anger', *Village Voice*, XXIV/50 (1979), p. 67.
10 Jean Baudrillard, *Simulacra and Simulation*, 1981, reprint, eleventh edition, trans. Sheila Faria Glaser (Ann Arbor, MI, 2004), p. 43.
11 Ibid., p. 45.
12 Philip B. Meggs, 'The Women Who Saved New York!', *Print*, XLIII/1 (1989), pp. 61–71, 163–4.

13 Raphael Samuel, *Theatres of Memory* (London, 1994), p. 95.

14 'Nixon Endorses Nostalgia After Seeing Nanette', *New York Times*
(5 August 1971), p. 17.

15 George W. S. Trow, 'Bobby Bison's Big Memory Offer', *New Yorker*, l/27
(1974), p. 27.

16 Archibald MacLeish, 'Why the Craze for "The Good Old Days"', *US News
and World Report*, LXXV/20 (1973), p. 72.

17 'Nixon Endorses Nostalgia', p. 17.

18 Gerald Clarke, 'The Meaning of Nostalgia', *Time*, XCVII/18 (1971), p. 77.

19 Jean Starobinski, 'The Idea of Nostalgia', *Diogenes*, LXIV (1966), p. 90.

20 Ibid., p. 10.

21 Fred Davis, *Yearning for Yesterday: A Sociology of Nostalgia* (New York, 1979).

22 Clive Barnes, 'No, No Nanette is Back Alive', *New York Times* (20 January
1971), p. 24.

23 Jameson, 'Nostalgia for the Present', p. 526.

24 Baudrillard, *Simulacra and Simulation*, p. 43.

25 Seth Schiesel, 'Once-Visionary Disney Calls the Future a Thing of the Past',
New York Times (23 February 1997), p. 24.

26 William Booth, 'Planet Mouse: At Disney's Tomorrowland the Future is a
Timid Creature', *Washington Post* (24 June 1998), D. 01.

27 Christopher Cornford, 'Cold Rice Pudding and Revisionism', *Design*,
CCXXXI (1968), p. 46.

28 Ibid., p. 48.

29 Clarke, 'The Meaning of Nostalgia', p. 77.

30 David Harvey, *The Condition of Postmodernity: An Enquiry into the Origins of
Cultural Change* (Oxford, 1989), p. vii.

31 Thomas Crow, 'Modernism and Mass Culture in the Visual Arts', in
Modernism and Modernity, ed. Benjamin H. D. Buchloh, Serge Guilbaut
and David Solkin (Halifax, Nova Scotia, 1983), p. 253.

32 Baudrillard, *Simulacra and Simulation*, p. 43.

33 Ibid.

34 Ibid., p. 44.

35 Ibid., p. 47.

One: When Art Nouveau Became New Again

1 Evelyn Waugh, 'Gaudí', *Architectural Review*, LXVII (1930), pp. 309–10.
2 George Orwell, *Homage to Catalonia* (New York, 1952), p. 225.
3 Waugh, 'Gaudí', p. 309.
4 Anthony D. Hippisley Coxe, 'Kinky Classics', p. 67.
5 Hilton Kramer, 'The Erotic Style: Reflections on the Exhibition of Art Nouveau', *Arts Magazine*, XXXIV (1960), p. 26.
6 Deborah Silverman, *Art Nouveau in Fin-de-Siècle France* (Berkeley, CA, 1989), pp. 232–42.
7 Anonymous, 'Pillory, L'Art Nouveau at South Kensington', *Architectural Review*, nos. 111/8 (1901), p. 104; and Judith Neiswander, '"Fantastic Malady" or Competitive Edge? English Outrage at the Art Nouveau in 1901', *Apollo*, n. s., CXXVIII (1988), pp. 310–13.
8 Anonymous, 'Pillory, L'Art Nouveau at South Kensington', p. 310.
9 Anonymous, 'L'Art Nouveau: What is It and What is Thought of It?', *Magazine of Art*, II (1904), pp. 211–12.
10 Lewis Mumford, 'The Wavy Line versus the Cube', *Architecture*, LXII (December 1930); reprinted in *Architectural Record*, CXXXV/1 (1964), p. 115.
11 John Betjeman, '1830–1930: Still Going Strong: Guide to the Recent History of Interior Decoration', *Architectural Review*, LXVII (1930), p. 238.
12 Aline B. Saarinen, 'Famous, Derided and Revived', *New York Times* (13 March 1955), p. X9.
13 Museum of Modern Art archives, Philip Johnson, exhibition notes to *Objects 1900 and Today*, 1 April–1 May 1933.
14 Anonymous, 'Exhibitions in New York: "Objects 1900 And Today"', *New Yorker*, I (1933), p. 10.
15 Alfred Barr, letter to Adeline Guimard, 23 May 1949, in Adeline Oppenheim file, New York Public Library, Manuscripts and Archives.
16 Nikolaus Pevsner, *Pioneers of the Modern Movement from William Morris to Walter Gropius* (London, 1936).
17 Salvador Dalí, 'Phenomenology of L'Angélus Paranoiac-Critical Activity Applied to the Secondary Phenomena'; reprinted in Haim Finkelstein,

Collected Writings of Salvador Dalí (New York, 1998), p. 10.

18 Salvador Dalí, 'De la beauté terrifiante et comestible, de l'architecture modern style', *Minotaure*, II?IV (1933), pp. 69–76.

19 Salvador Dalí, 'L'Ane pourri', in *La Femme visible* (Paris, 1930), pp 19–20.

20 Dalí, 'De la beauté terrifiante et comestible', p. 71.

21 Dalí, 'De la beauté terrifiante et comestible', pp. 69–76.

22 A. Galvano, 'Un arredamento di Carlo Mollino', *Stile*, V–VI (1941), pp. 31–42.

23 Kenneth Fehrman, *Postwar Interior Design, 1945–1960* (New York, 1986), p. 72.

24 Hermand Jost, *Jugendstil* (Darmstadt, 1971), p. 4.

25 'Neo-Liberty: The Debate', *The Architectural Review* CXXX (1959), p. 343.

26 Reyner Banham, 'Neoliberty: The Retreat from Modern Architecture', *Architectural Review*, CXXV (1959), p. 235.

27 'Neo-Liberty: The Debate', p. 343.

28 Banham, 'Neoliberty', p. 235.

29 John M. Jacobus, Jr, 'Review of Steven Tschudi Madsen', *Sources of Art Nouveau*, *Art Bulletin*, XV (1958), p. 373.

30 Ibid.

31 Saarinen, 'Famous, Derided and Revived', p. X9.

32 Herbert Weissberger, 'After Many Years: Tiffany Glass', *Carnegie Magazine*, XXX (1956), p. 279.

33 Steven Bruce, interview with the author, New York, 21 February 2001.

34 Calvin Tomkins, 'Raggedy Andy', in *Andy Warhol*, ed. John Coplans (Greenwich, CT, 1970), p. 9.

35 Saarinen, 'Famous, Derided and Revived', p. X9.

36 Cynthia Kellogg, 'Design by Mr Tiffany', *New York Times Magazine* (26 January 1958), p. 50.

37 Betty Pepis, 'Revival of Tiffany Lamps Empties Attics and Closets', *New York Times* (9 July 1956), p. 28.

38 Ettore Sottsass, 'Liberty: la biblia di mezzo secolo', *Domus*, CCXCII (1954), p. 43.

39 Edgar Kaufmann, 'Tiffany: Then and Now', *Interiors*, CXIV (1955), p. 82.

40 Ibid., p. 84.

41 Saarinen, 'Famous, Derided and Revived', p. X9.

42 Steven Bruce, interview with author, New York, 21 February 2001.

43 Anonymous, 'After Hours', *Harpers*, CCXIII (1956), p. 80.

44 John Canady, 'Art Nouveau', *New York Times* (12 June 1960), p. 131.

45 Susan Sontag, 'Notes on Camp', in *A Susan Sontag Reader* (New York, 1982), p. 118.

46 Ibid., p. 108

47 Ibid., p. 107.

48 Ned Rorem, *Knowing When to Stop: A Memoir* (New York, 1994), p. 470.

49 Saarinen, 'Famous, Derided and Revived', p. X9.

50 Sontag, 'Notes on Camp', pp. 117, 105.

51 Anonymous, 'New Look at Art Nouveau', *Time*, LXXXIV/8 (1964), p. 63.

52 Ibid., p. 10.

53 Advertisement for Stern's department store, *New York Times* (14 March 1965), p. 55.

54 Anonymous, 'New Look at Art Nouveau', p. 63.

55 Anonymous, 'Nouveau Frisco', *Time*, LXXXIX/14 (1967), p. 66.

56 Gloria Steinem, 'The Ins and Outs of Pop Culture', *Life*, LIX/8 (1965), p. 80

57 George Melly, *Revolt into Style: The Pop Arts* (London, 1971), p. 150.

58 Anonymous, 'After Hours', p. 80.

59 Anonymous, 'Art Nouveau: Then and Now', *Print*, XVIII (1964), p. 17.

60 Ernest Hoch, 'Revivals, Sterility and Riotous Self-Expression', *Studio International*, CLXXV (1968), p. 219.

61 Thomas Frank, *The Conquest of Cool: Business Culture, Counterculture and Hip Consumerism* (Chicago, 1998).

62 Hoch, 'Revivals, Sterility and Riotous Self-Expression', p. 219.

63 Anonymous, 'Nouveau Frisco', p. 69.

64 Ibid.

65 Carl Belz, 'Around the Bay', *Art International*, XI/3 (1967), p. 49.

66 Anonymous, 'Nouveau Frisco', p. 69.

67 Paul Grushkin, *The Art of Rock: Posters from Presley to Punk* (New York, 1987), p. 72.

68 Anonymous, 'Nouveau Frisco', p. 69.

69 Jon Borgzinner, 'The Great Poster Wave', *Life*, LXIII/9 (1967), p. 42.

70 Anonymous, 'Nouveau Frisco', p. 69.

71 Ibid.

72 Grushkin, *The Art of Rock*, p. 87.

73 Anonymous, 'Nouveau Frisco', p. 69.

Two: *Moderne* Times

1 Salvador Dalí, 'How an Elvis Presley Becomes a Roy Lichtenstein', *Arts*, XLI/6 (1967), p. 26.

2 John Coplans, 'Roy Lichtenstein: An Interview', *Roy Lichtenstein*, exh. cat., Pasadena Art Museum (Pasadena, CA, 1967), p. 16.

3 Arthur Drexler and Greta Daniel, *Introduction to Twentieth-Century Design: From the Collection of the Museum of Modern Art* (New York, 1959), p. 4.

4 Sigfried Giedion, *A Decade of New Architecture* (Zurich, 1951), p. 3.

5 Gloria Steinem, 'The Ins and Outs of Pop Culture', p. 80.

6 Hilary Gelson, 'Art Deco', *Times* [London] (12 November 1966), p. 13.

7 Edgar Kaufmann, Review of Martin Battersby, 'The Decorative Twenties, Style and Design, 1901–1929', and Giulia Veronesi, 'Stile 1925: ascesa e caduta delle "Arts Déco"', *Art Bulletin*, LII/3 (1970), Section CII, p. 340.

8 Christopher Neve, 'Ah, Before the War . . . Changing Attitudes to Art Deco', *Country Life*, CL/3866 (1971), p. 146.

9 Jean W. Progner, 'Art Deco: Anatomy of a Revival', *Print*, XXV/I (1971), p. 28.

10 Bevis Hillier, *Art Deco of the '20s and '30s* (London, 1968), p. 158.

11 Natalie Gittelson, 'Art Deco: Phase Two', *Harper's Bazaar*, MMMCXXXI (1972), p. 118.

12 Janet Malcolm, 'On and Off the Avenue: About the House', *New Yorker*, CLXXII/10 (1971), p. 111.

13 Elayne Rapping, *The Movie of the Week: Private Stories/Public Events* (Minneapolis, MN, 1992), pp. 11–12.

14 Lawrence Alloway, 'Roy Lichtenstein's Period Style: From the Thirties to

the Sixties and Back', *Arts*, XVII/1 (1967), p. 27.

15   Hillier, *Art Deco of the 20s and 30s*, p. 165.

16   Malcolm, 'On And Off the Avenue', p. 114.

17   Alloway, 'Roy Lichtenstein's Period Style', p. 25.

18   David Bourdon, 'Stacking the Deco', *New York Magazine*, VII/45 (1974), p. 66.

19   Natalie Gittelson, 'Art Deco: Phase Two', p. 118.

20   Ibid.

21   Ibid., p. 119.

22   Ibid., p. 118.

23   Andy Warhol and Pat Hakett, *POPism: The Warhol '60s* (New York, 1980), p. 65.

24   Jeanne Siegel, 'Thoughts on the "Modern" Period', in *Roy Lichtenstein*, ed. John Coplans (New York, 1972), p. 94.

25   Alloway, 'Roy Lichtenstein's Period Style', p. 27.

26   Siegel, 'Thoughts on the "Modern" Period', p. 93.

27   Ibid., p. 94.

28   Paul Katz, 'Roy Lichtenstein . . . Modern Sculpture with Velvet Rope', *Art Now: New York*, I/1 (January 1969), n. p.

29   Alloway, 'Roy Lichtenstein's Period Style', p. 25.

30   Katz, 'Roy Lichtenstein . . . Modern Sculpture with Velvet Rope', n. p.

31   Sidney Tillim, 'Lichtenstein's Sculpture', *Artforum*, VI/5 (1968), p. 24.

32   Robert Rosenblum, 'Frank Stella', *Penguin New Art I* (Harmondsworth, 1970), p. 50.

33   Robert Smithson, 'Ultramoderne', *Arts*, XLII/1 (1967), p. 31.

34   Ibid.

35   Sol LeWitt, 'Ziggurats: Liberating Set-backs to Architectural Fashion', *Arts*, XLI/1 (1966), pp. 24–5.

36   Smithson, 'Ultramoderne', p. 33.

37   See Pamela Lee, 'Ultramoderne: or, How George Kubler Stole the Time in Sixties Art', in *Chronophobia* (Cambridge, MA, 2005), pp. 218–56.

38   Smithson, 'Ultramoderne', p. 32.

39   Ibid., p. 31.

40   Ibid., p. 33.

41 Ibid.

42 Alwyn Turner, *Biba: The Biba Experience* (London, 2004), p. 48.

43 Marvin D. Schwartz, 'Art Nouveau, and Art Deco, the Avant-Garde Antiques', *ARTnews*, LXXI/8 (1972), p. 62.

44 Tillim, 'Lichtenstein's Sculpture', p. 23.

45 'Why the Craze for the "Good Old Days"', *US News and World Report*, LXXXV/20, p. 72.

46 Anne Hollander, 'Art Deco's Back and New York's Got It', *New York*, XVII/45 (1974), p. 54.

47 Gerald Clarke, 'The Meaning of Nostalgia', *Time*, XCVII/19 (1971), p. 77.

48 Hollander, 'Art Deco's Back and New York's Got It', p. 54.

49 Progner, 'Art Deco: Anatomy of a Revival', p. 27.

50 Hollander, 'Art Deco's Back and New York's Got It', p. 54.

51 Clarke, 'The Meaning of Nostalgia', p. 77.

52 Lesley Hornby aka Twiggy, *Twiggy* (New York, 1968), p. 121.

53 Hollander, 'Art Deco's Back and New York's Got It', p. 54.

54 John Canaday, 'Art Deco in Minneapolis: No Sir, That Ain't My Baby Now', *New York Times* (1971), D21.

55 Clarke, 'The Meaning of Nostalgia', p. 77.

56 Progner, 'Art Deco: Anatomy of a Revival', p. 36.

57 Clarke, 'The Meaning of Nostalgia', p. 77.

58 Progner, 'Art Deco: Anatomy of a Revival', p. 28.

59 Ibid., p. 36.

60 Ernest Hoch, 'Revivals, Sterility and Riotous Self-Expression', *Studio International*, CLXXV (1968), pp. 222, 221.

61 Progner, 'Art Deco: Anatomy of a Revival', p. 32.

62 Ibid., p. 35.

63 Lawrence Alloway, 'Art', *The Nation*, CCXIII/4 (1971), p. 124.

64 Gittelson, 'Art Deco: Phase Two', p. 118.

65 Robert Pincus-Witten, 'Art Deco', *Artforum*, IX/4 (1970), p. 71.

Three: Fabricated Fifties

1 'True Grease', *Time*, CXIX/22 (1972), p. 56.

2 Jack Kroll, 'Before "Hair"', *Newsweek*, LXXIX/2 (1972), p. 95.

3 Frank Heath, 'Nostalgia Shock', *Saturday Review*, LIV (1971), p. 19.

4 Tony Wilson, 'Haley, Perkins, Eddy, Everlys – Suddenly in Britain It's Rock', *Melody Maker*, XLIII (1968), p. 1.

5 'Teddy Boys, 1970: Slowly Rocking on . . .', *Sunday Times Magazine* (27 September 1970), p. 23.

6 Ibid.

7 Dick Hebdige, *Subculture: The Meaning of Style* (London, 1976), p. 46.

8 Jonathan Rodgers, 'Back to the '50s', *Newsweek*, LXXIX (1972), p. 78.

9 'The Nifty Fifties', *Life* (18 June 1972), p. 38.

10 'R 'n' R Revival Rides High', *Billboard*, LXXXIII (18 September 1971), p. 1.

11 Joel Vance, 'Hy Whu-hawnt You Hy Nee-heed You', *New York Times* (23 January 1972), p. D26.

12 George J. Leonard and Robert Leonard, 'Sha Na Na and the Woodstock Generation', *Columbia College Today* (1989), p. 28.

13 Ibid., p. 28.

14 Rodgers, 'Back to the '50s', p. 79.

15 'Sha Na Na Star Trades Gold Lame Suit for Pinstripes', *Associated Press* (1 July 1998).

16 Stephen Farber, '"Graffiti" Ranks with *Bonnie and Clyde*', *New York Times* (5 August 1973), p. 97.

17 Rodgers, 'Back to the '50s', p. 80.

18 Richard Horn, *Fifties Style: Then and Now* (Philadelphia, 1985), p. 8.

19 Shaun Considine, '"Grease" Slides into its Fifth Year', *New York Times* (15 February 1976), p. D5.

20 'The Nifty Fifties', p. 39.

21 Kroll, 'Before "Hair"', p. 95.

22 'The Nifty Fifties', p. 42.

23 Andrew H. Malcolm, 'Students Revive the Good Ole '50s', *New York Times* (17 May 1971), p. 1.

24 'Fabulous '50s', *Time*, CII/8 (1973), p. 58.

25 Rodgers, 'Back to the '50s', p. 78.

26 'True Grease', p. 10.

27 Kroll, 'Before "Hair"', p. 95.

28 Douglas Miller and Marion Nowak, *The Fifties: The Way They Really Were* (Garden City, NY, 1977), p. 5.

29 Rita Reif, 'After Art Nouveau, It's Art Deco Once Again', *New York Times* (20 October 1970), p. 50.

30 Leonard and Leonard, 'Sha Na Na and the Woodstock Generation', p. 28.

31 Malcolm, 'Students Revive the Good Ole '50s', p. 1.

32 Edith Oliver, 'Off Broadway', *New Yorker* XLVIII (1972), p. 68.

33 'Back to the '50s', p. 78.

34 Eric Goldman, 'Good-Bye to the '50s – and Good Riddance', *Harper's Magazine*, X/220 (1960), pp. 27–9.

35 Ronald Berman, *America in the Sixties: An Intellectual History* (New York, 1968), pp. 1–8.

36 Heath, 'Nostalgia Shock', p. 19.

37 Bevis Hillier, 'Review of Richard Horn, *Fifties Style: Then and Now*', *Los Angeles Times Magazine* (16 February 1986), p. 20.

38 Gerald Clarke, 'The Meaning of Nostalgia', *Time*, XCVII/19 (1971), p. 77.

39 Stefan Kanfer 'Back to the Unfabulous '50s', *Time*, CVI (1974), p. 56.

40 Richard R. Lingeman, 'There Was Another Fifties', *New York Times Magazine* (17 June 1973), p. 24.

41 'True Grease', p. 56.

42 Oliver, 'Off Broadway', p. 68.

43 Vance, 'Hy Whu-hawnt You Hy Nee-heed You', p. D26.

44 Malcolm, 'Students Revive the Good Ole 1950s', p. 1

45 'The Instant Decade', *Horizon Magazine*, XIV/1 (1972), pp. 2–3.

46 Alan Morris, *Collaboration and Resistance Reviewed: Writers and the 'Mode Retro' in Post-Gaullist France* (Oxford, 1992), p. 85.

47 Naomi Greene, *Landscapes of Loss: The Nationalist Past in Postwar French Cinema* (Princeton, NJ, 1999), p. 65.

48 Nan Robertson, 'The New War Movies That Say "J'Accuse" To the French',

New York Times (14 October 1974), p. 2.

49 Ibid.

50 Bernadine Morris, 'Now Why Art They Throwing Brickbats at Saint Laurent?', *New York Times* (2 February 1971), p. 42.

51 'Saint Laurent Retorts', *New York Times* (19 February 1971), p. 30.

52 Bernadine Morris, 'Saint Laurent, Ungaro and Dior – Many Studies, No New Look', *New York Times* (24 July 1970), p. 37.

53 'Saint Laurent Retorts', p. 30.

54 Michel Capdenac, 'Révolte dévoyée, film fourvoyé', *Europe*, DXL/DXLI (1974), p. 267.

55 Malcolm, 'Students Revive the Good Ole '50s', p. 1.

56 Jean Baudrillard, *Simulacra and Simulation* (Ann Arbor, MI, 1994), pp. 43–8.

57 P.M.S., 'Book review of Alan Hess, *Googie: Fifties Coffee Shop Architecture*', *Architectural Record* CLXXVI/6 (1986), p. 71

58 'Putting on the Fifties Style', *Sunday Times Magazine* (31 October 1976), p. 10.

59 Ibid., p. 10.

60 'Back to the '50s', p. 78.

61 Kim Levin, 'Fifties Fallout The Hydrogen Juke Box', *Arts* XLVIII (1974), p. 29.

62 Ibid.

63 Ibid., p. 30.

64 Ibid., p. 29.

65 Marc Arcenaux, *The Atomic Age* (San Francisco, 1975), p. 5.

66 Nayana Currimbhoy, 'Book review of Alan Hess, *Googie: Fifties Coffee Shop Architecture*', *Interiors*, CXLVI (1987), p. 21.

67 Ibid., p. 22.

68 Alan Hess, *Googie: Fifties Coffee Shop Architecture* (San Francisco, 1986), p. 10.

69 Karen Schoemer, 'At Home in the Top 40 and Still Full of Kitsch', *New York Times* (31 December 1989), p. H27.

70 Lance Morrow, 'Dreaming of the Eisenhower Years', *Time*, CXVI/4 (1980), p. 33.

71 Horn, *Fifties Style Then and Now*, p. 165.

72 Jed Perl, 'Book Review of Martin Eidelberg, *Design, 1935–1965: What Modern Was*', *New Republic* CCVI/14 (1992), p. 28.

73 Horn, *Fifties Style*, p. 165.

Four: The Lure of Yesterday's Tomorrows

1   Paula Scher, 'Back in the USSR (Or that Ukraine Type Really Knocks Me Out)', p. 257.

2   Ibid.

3   Ibid.

4   James R. Mellow, 'The Bauhaus is Alive and Well in Soup Plates and Skyscrapers', *New York Times Magazine* (14 September 1969), p. 24.

5   K. A. Jelenski, 'Avant-Garde and Revolution', *Arts*, XXV/1 (1960), p. 36.

6   Paul Wood, 'The Politics of the Avant-Garde', *The Great Utopia*, exh. cat., Guggenheim Museum (New York, 1992), p. 1.

7   Hilton Kramer, 'Artists of the Soviet Utopia', *New York Times* (19 September 1971), p. D23.

8   A. Alvarez, 'With a Hole in Its Heart', *New York Times* (14 March 1971), p. D19.

9   Oleg Shvidkovsky, 'Art in Revolution', *Art in Revolution: Soviet Art and Design since 1917*, exh. cat., Hayward Gallery (London, 1971), p. 18.

10 Kramer, 'Artists of the Soviet Utopia', p. D23.

11 Scher, 'Back in the USSR', p. 257.

12 Peter Schjeldahl, 'The Eye of the Revolution', *Art in America*, LXIX (1981), p. 91.

13 Christopher Wilson, 'David King', *Eye*, XII/48 (2003), p. 65.

14 Rick Poynor, 'The Man Who Saved History', *Print*, CII/52, issue 6 (1998), p. 56.

15 Wilson, 'David King', p. 62.

16 Simon Frith, Simon and Howard Horne, *Art into Pop*, (New York, 1987), p 60.

17 Nick de Ville, *Album: Style and Image in Sleeve Design* (London, 2003), p. 161.

18 Jon Wozencroft, *Brody: The Graphic Language of Neville Brody* (London, 1988), p. 133.

19 William Taylor, 'Message and Muscle: An Interview with Swatch Titan Nicolas Hayek', *Harvard Business Review*, LXXI/2 (1993), p. 98.

20 Isadore Barmash, 'Prospects', *New York Times* (9 September 1984), p. F1.

21 Philip Meggs, 'The Women Who Saved New York!', *Print*, XLIII/1 (1989), pp. 61–71; 163–4.

22 Ibid., p. 61.

23 Patricia Sellers, 'Do You Need Your Ad Agency?', *Fortune*, CXXVIII/12 (1993), p. 147.

24 Scher, 'Back in the USSR', p. 257.

25 Ibid.

26 Paula Scher, *Make It Bigger* (New York, 2002), p. 51.

27 Joshua Levine, 'Why "New" Is Old Hat', *Forbes*, CXLVIII/2 (1991), p. 302.

28 Sarah Mower, 'Style: Retro Mania/Design Trends in 1987', *Guardian* (8 January 1987), p. 10.

29 Hilary De Vries, 'Retro-Chic and Other Big Trends: A Guide to Ins and Outs', *Christian Science Monitor* (20 January 1987), p. 10.

30 Philip Meggs, 'Mondrian as a Marketing Tool', *AIGA Journal of Graphic Design*, VIII/2 (1990), p. 13.

31 Rick Poynor, 'Black and White and Red All Over', *Design*, CDLXX (1988), p. 52.

32 Wood, 'The Politics of the Avant-Garde', p. 1.

33 Poynor, 'Black and White and Red All Over', p. 52.

34 Jean Baudrillard, *Simulacra and Simulation* (Ann Arbor, MI, 2004), p. 43.

35 Tibor Kalman, J. Abbott Miller and Carrie Jacobs, 'Good History, Bad History', *Print*, XLV/2 (1991), p. 115.

36 Ibid., p. 119.

37 Claudia Deutsch, 'Swatch Catches Up with Itself', *New York Times* (16 August 1987), p. F4.

38 Scher, *Make It Bigger*, p. 98.

39 Kalman, Miller and Jacobs, 'Good History, Bad History', p. 120.

40 Paul Rand, Introduction, in *Herbert Matter: A Retrospective*, exh. cat., A&A

Gallery, School of Art, Yale University (New Haven, CT, 1978), n. p.

41 Kalman, Miller and Jacobs, 'Good History, Bad History', p. 121.

42 Rand, Introduction, n.

43 Kalman, Miller and Jacobs, 'Good History, Bad History', p. 23.

44 Michael Davie, *In the Future Now: A Report from California* (London, 1972), p. 225.

45 Martin E. Marty, 'Looking Backward Into the Future', *New York Times* (6 February 1975), p. 33.

46 Natalie Gittelson, 'Art Deco: Phase Two', *Harper's Bazaar*, MMMCXXXII (1972), p. 118.

47 Peter Plagens, 'The Groupie and the Commissar: Revolutionary Posters and Capitalist Billboards', *Artforum*, XIII/ (1975), p. 61.

48 Scher, 'Back in the USSR', p. 237.

49 Nayana Currimbhoy, 'Review of Alan Hess, *Googie: Fifties Coffee Shop Architecture*', *Interiors*, CXLVI (1987), p. 22.

50 Paul Richard, 'The Retro Art Renaissance: To See is To Remember', *Washington Post* (16 October 1977), p. G3.

51 Ibid.

Epilogue

1 James Laver, *Taste and Fashion* (London, 1937), ch. 18.

2 Paula Scher, 'Back in the USSR (Or that Ukraine Type Really Knocks Me Out)', p. 257.

3 Tom Appelo, 'The Future Isn't What It Used to Be', *Los Angeles Times* (4 January 1998), p. 4.

4 William Booth, 'Planet Mouse, At Disney's New Tomorrowland The Future Is a Timid Creature', *Washington Post* (24 June 1998), p. D1.

5 Daryl Strickland, 'With Tomorrowland, Disneyland Bets That the Future is Now', *St Louis Post-Dispatch* (17 May 1998), p. T3.

Select Bibliography
and Filmography

Art into Life: Russian Constructivism, 1914–1932 (Seattle, WA, 1990)

Barthes, Roland, *Camera Lucida: Reflections on Photography* (London, 1982)

—, *The Responsibility of Forms: Critical Essays on Music, Art and Representation*, trans. R. Howard (Oxford, 1986)

—, *Roland Barthes by Roland Barthes* (Berkeley, CA, 1994)

Baudrillard, Jean, *Simulacra and Simulation* (Ann Arbor, MI, 2004)

—, ed., Mark Poster, *Selected Writings* (Stanford, CA, 1988)

Buchloh, Benjamin H. D., Serge Guilbaut and David Solkin, eds, *Modernism and Modernity* (Halifax, Nova Scotia, 1983)

Corn, Joseph C., and Brian Horrigan, *Yesterday's Tomorrows: Past Visions of the American Future* (Baltimore, MD, 1984)

Davis, Fred, *Yearning for Yesterday: A Sociology of Nostalgia* (New York, 1979)

Flam, Jack, ed., *Robert Smithson: The Collected Writings* (Berkeley, CA, 1996)

Frank, Thomas, *The Conquest of Cool: Business Culture, Counterculture and Hip Consumerism* (Chicago, 1998)

Gebhard, David, 'The Moderne in the US, 1920–1941', *Architectural Association Quarterly*, II/3 (July 1970), pp. 4–20

Grainge, Paul, 'TIME's Past in the Present: Nostalgia and the Black and White Image', *Journal of American Studies*, XXXIII/3 (1999), pp. 383–92

—, 'Advertising the Archive: Nostalgia and the (Post)national Imaginary', *American Studies*, XV/2–3 (2000), pp. 137–57

—, *Monochrome Memories: Nostalgia and Style in Retro America* (Westport, CT, 2002)

—, 'Nostalgia and Style in Retro America: Moods, Modes and Media Recycling', *Journal of American and Comparative Cultures*, XXIII/1 (2000), pp. 27–34

The Great Utopia: the Russian and Soviet Avant-Garde, 1915–1932 (New York, 1992)

Greene, Naomi, *Landscapes of Loss: The Nationalist Past in Postwar French Cinema* (Princeton, NJ, 1999)

Greenhalgh, Paul, ed., *Modernism in Design* (London, 1990)

Gregson, Nicky, Kate Brooks and Louise Crewe, 'Bjorn Again? Rethinking 70s Revivalism Through the Reappropriation of 70s Clothing', *Fashion Theory*, V/1 (2001), pp. 3–27

Harvey, David, *The Condition of Postmodernity: An Enquiry into the Origins of Cultural Change* (Oxford, 1989)

Heller, Steven, and Julie Lasky, *Borrowed Design: Use and Abuse of Historical Form* (New York, 1993)

—, and Louise Fili, *Typology: Type design from the Victorian Era to the Digital Age* (New York, 1999)

Jackson, Lesley, *The Sixties: Decade of Design Revolution* (London, 1991)

Jameson, Fredric, 'Nostalgia for the Present', *South Atlantic Quarterly*, LXXXVIII/2 (1989), pp. 517–37

—, *Postmodernism: or, The Cultural Logic of Late Capitalism* (Durham, NC, 1991)

Kalman, Tibor, J. Abbott Miller and Carrie Jacobs, 'Good History, Bad History', *Print*, XLV/2 (1991), pp. 114–35

Lippard, Lucy, *Get the Message?: A Decade of Art for Social Change* (New York, 1984)

Lupton, Ellen, *Design, Writing, Research: Writing on Graphic Design* (New York, 1996)

Meggs, Philip B., 'The Women Who Saved New York!', *Print*, XLIII/1 (1989), pp. 61–71

Morris, Alan, *Collaboration and Resistance Reviewed: Writers and the 'Mode Retro' in Post-Gaullist France* (Oxford, 1992)

Nora, Pierre, *Realms of Memory* (New York, 1996)

Progner, Jean, 'Art Deco: Anatomy of a Revival', *Print*, XVI/1 (1971)

Samuel, Raphael, *Theatres of Memory* (London, 1994)

Sontag, Susan, *Susan Sontag Reader* (New York, 1982)

Starobinski, Jean, 'The Idea of Nostalgia', *Diogenes*, LXIV (1966), pp. 81–103

Tannock, Stuart, 'Nostalgia Critique', *Cultural Studies*, IX/3 (1995), pp. 453–64

Whitely, Nigel, *Pop Design: Modernism to Mod* (London, 1987)

American Graffiti, dir. George Lucas, 1973

The Boy Friend, dir. Ken Russell, 1971

Blade Runner, dir. Ridley Scott, 1982

Bonnie and Clyde, dir. Arthur Penn, 1967

Lacombe Lucien, dir. Louis Malle, 1974

My Fair Lady, dir. George Cukor, 1964

Star Wars, dir. George Lucas, 1977

Acknowledgements

In writing this book, I'd like to thank many for their tips, advice, encouragement and helpful criticism, including Stephanie Acton, Stephen Bruce, Eric Carlson, Tracy Fitzpatrick, Louise Fili, Carma Gorman, Adam Halvorson, Steven Heller, Aya Kato, Joy Kestenbaum, Jane Kromm, Maud Lavin, Michael Lobel, Amy Ogata, Rosalie Reutershan and Gabe Weisberg. I am also grateful to the libraries whose collections I've used, including Columbia University, Cooper Union Lubaliin, New York Public Library, Purchase College and the University of California. For our fruitful discussions and their often astute observations, I'd also like to thank my students. Additional thanks to Catherine Bindman and Elizabeth Franzen. At Reaktion, I'd like to credit Vivian Constantinopoulos and Michael Leaman. The support of my parents George and Mary Ellen has been invaluable. And, most of all, I'd like to thank my husband Matt for his sharp eye, generous time and ready comments.

Photo Acknowledgements

The author and publishers wish to express their thanks to the below sources of illustrative material and/or permission to reproduce it:

Photo © Advertising Archives: p. 92; photo AFP © Getty Images: p. 121; photo courtesy of *Art in America:* p. 45; photos Art Resources: pp. 36, 39; photo Ballard © Getty Images: p. 101; photo Alan Band, Hulton Archive/Getty Images: p. 23; photos © Bettmann Archives/Corbis: pp. 62, 74, 110 (foot); photo Charles Bonnay, Time & Life Pictures/Getty Images: p. 54; image courtesy of Neville Brody: p. 139; photo courtesy of Stephen Bruce: p. 46; © Corbis: pp. 130, 154; photo Evans, © Hulton Archives/Getty Images: p. 164; photos *Evening Standard,* © Getty Images: pp. 89, 107; photo courtesy of Louise Fili: p. 146; photo courtesy of Gagosian Gallery © ARS: p. 157; image courtesy of Milton Glaser: p. 55; © Lynn Goldsmith/Corbis: p. 129; photo Henry Groskinsky, Time & Life Pictures/Getty Images: p. 66; photos © Hulton Archive/Getty Images: pp. 93, 99; photo © Hulton-Deutsch Collection/Corbis: p. 87; photo Yale Joel © Getty Images: p. 110 (top); photo Keystone, Hulton Archive/Getty Images: p. 11; photo courtesy of David King: p. 138; photo © Douglas Kirkland/Corbis: p. 90; artwork concept Ralf Hutter Florian Schneider, © Kraftwerk/Astralwerks: p. 140; photo © Estate of Roy